UP

LESSONS OF ADVERSITY,
HITTING BOTTOM,
AND CHOOSING
A LIFE
THAT MATTERS

JAKE WIDMANN

WISE INK CREATIVE PUBLISHING

ISBN 13: 978-1-63489-166-0

Library of Congress Catalog Number: 2018956826

Printed in the United States of America

First Printing: 2018

22　21　20　19　18　　5　4　3　2　1

Cover design by Nupoor Gordon

Wise Ink Creative Publishing replaces every tree used in printing their books by planting thousands of trees every year in reforestation programs. Learn more at wiseink.com.

CONTENTS

"I don't want to get to the end of my life and find that I just lived the length of it. I want to have lived the width of it as well."

Diane Ackerman

INTRODUCTION

Are we all meant to live a life of greatness—or, at the very least, a life absent of most adversity and suffering? How can we best navigate life so as to remain true to ourselves while still entertaining advice and guidance from those who care about us? Why do we do the things we do? How much do our actions affect others? How do we resist temptations in the face of difficult times when all we want is something to ease the pain? How could we ever leave our current circle of friends in search of the life we truly want? What on earth are we supposed to do with our lives? Is patience really that necessary to achieve our goals? Can we actually go from where we are to where we want to be, or is that just something people say? Is there truly more out there for our life than what we're currently experiencing?

Take a few minutes to think briefly about these things. No need to write down your answers—just a few quick thoughts on each question will do.

When I was much younger, I remember being told countless times, in a variety of ways, to stop asking so many questions. I suppose it's fitting, then, that I turn around and begin this book by asking a litany of questions. Questions that I hope to answer throughout this book or, at minimum, make you think more deeply about.

You may have been a curious kid as well. I'd say it's safe to assume that you were curious about this book and the content within it. You picked it up wondering if it was just another self-help book, or maybe the cover caught your eye. Or, possibly, your life is a living hell and you thought this book might help you. In any case, your life is somewhere along the spectrum from living hell to the existence you actually want, and you hoped that this book would help you position yourself a little closer to the latter. No matter why you grabbed it, I promise to make the time you spend reading it worthwhile. That is, if you'll do the work required to overcome your adversity, build some resiliency, and improve your life.

Let me quickly say this: I began writing this book in hopes of helping people navigate their lives in a way that allowed them to avoid adversity—to never experience it at all. Then, while writing it and reflecting on everything I had gone through, I realized how imperative every event I experienced was in shaping the person I am today. What began as a book about avoiding adversity transitioned into a book about avoiding *some* adversity—but also a book that would help people navigate through adversity and extract every bit of value from it that they could.

For me, some of those opening questions were easy to answer; others not so much. I'm sure the same was true for you. There were probably some distinct people that came to mind, maybe a few certain places and memories as well. Those will not be the only questions I'll ask you as you continue reading. Some are integrated directly into the text, but many of them can be found in the accompanying guide, which was built specifically for this book and for anyone who knows there is more to life than what they're currently living but isn't exactly sure how to obtain it. You can find it at www.sologood.co/bookresources.

In answering those questions, I need you to do something: be honest with yourself. Don't try to answer them to make yourself feel better about a choice that you made. Don't answer them in a way that allows you to continue avoiding your pain. Be open with yourself. Be vulnerable with this book in your hands. Be the man or woman you want to be instead of the one you've needed to be in order to meet your needs and survive your past.

I know I'm asking a lot from you only a couple pages in, but you want a profoundly better life, right? Being honest and humble means you need to admit that you weren't right all of the time. It requires that you face the pain in your life rather than run from it. I know as well as anyone that it's not fun to admit fault and undergo the process of changing, but it's damn worth it in the long run.

As my old football coaches and drill sergeants would say, "I'm not asking you to do anything I have not done myself at some point." I know how hard it is, but I also know that you're capable of doing it.

By reading and implementing the content within this book, I can confidently say that you will have begun journeying to a much better place mentally, emotionally, and likely physically. You will begin to carry yourself differently because you will have greater confidence in yourself and your future and a great sense of self-awareness. You'll know with greater certainty what you want and how to obtain it, and understand what held you back from obtaining it in the past. I know all of this might seem pretty hard to believe at this point, depending on how dire your situation is, but you need to realize that your journey of going from where you are to where you want to be has only just begun. The lessons ahead will remain with you, and you'll be able to implement them long after you have closed this book, much like I still am today. This is your life, and as long as you're wanting to improve it, the content ahead will remain mostly relevant.

To all but guarantee its relevance, I did my fair share of research and work before and during the writing of this book. Over the years I've read several other books, including *The Subtle Art of Not Giving a F*ck* by Mark Manson, which you will either love or hate, mostly depending on your ability to tolerate a lot of F-bombs. He said, "We all have our chosen methods to numb the pain of our problems, and in moderate doses there is nothing wrong with this. But the longer we avoid and the longer we numb, the more painful it will be when we finally do confront our issues." *Oh, how true this is,* I thought when I stopped to ponder those words a little longer. If your life is ever going to get better, you're going to have to deal with your chosen method of numbing the pain—whatever it may be.

Sure, you can allow your problems to persist and choose to ignore them like I did for so many years, but as you'll learn, there's only one thing guaranteed by taking that route: continuing to get what you've been getting. Aren't you sick of the same old result? Isn't that, at least partially, why you picked up this book?

Adversity, as I'll share more about later on, can take on infinite forms. For me, it was alcoholism and the decisions I made while under its influence. For you, it might be any form of addiction: gambling, food, sex, technology, cigarettes, etc. It could be a total downfall after a bad breakup or divorce. It could be the death of a loved one or an unfortunate medical diagnosis. Whatever it may be, the pages ahead will surely help you through it.

All of the elements of my downfall and climb out of rock bottom have given me a unique perspective. A perspective that lit a fire inside of me to help as many people as possible end their suffering, overcome their adversity, and live a life that matters. (That last part is up to you to define.) I know through my personal experiences, my conversations with friends, and other random encounters that life can be unexpectedly flipped upside down and made to look like the opposite of what we once dreamt of. What that personal experience, those conversations, and life in general have taught me is that we often remain oblivious to the fact that it's mostly our own doing that delivers us to an undesirable place.

The pages that lie ahead will take you through my journey to rock bottom and back. In this book, I share everything I learned along the way, including the key elements to overcoming adversity and why taking full ownership over your life is a requirement. That's where you'll find immense freedom.

The things that qualify me to write this book are my gradual descent into and climb out of alcoholism and my will to never give up. Every unthinkable story and every ridiculous choice I made—the endless blackouts; countless times driving drunk; drugs used; lies told; disagreements with parents, friends, and coworkers; close calls with cops; days spent in jail; fines paid; and much more—gave me the opportunity to learn valuable lessons. But I also learned from the smart choices I made—my desire to change, the books I read, my conversations with friends and strangers, my hard work, my good luck, the counseling sessions I attended, my willingness to fail, my trust in the process, my patience, my belief that there was more for my life, my investment in good relationships, my refusal to give up hope, and my sacrifice of "fun" for a better, healthier life. That's what gives my words value and meaning, enabling you to trust and believe that what I have written here is for your benefit.

During my conversations over the years, I've observed a central theme in my own story and in the stories of others. Those who have made it out of rock bottom or past adversity have done so on the back of hope or belief that there was more for their life than what they were currently experiencing. If you can maintain those two things, you're already doing well for yourself. Honestly.

What's not in the following pages is some twelve-step program that, once completed, will reward you with a perfectly laid path to the life you've always wanted. You may know me well, or this may be the first time you're hearing of me, but I'm not a doctor, psychologist, therapist, or anything in between. I'm a guy who cares a whole hell of a lot about people, believes in the insane power of each and every one of our individual lives and stories, and hopes that he can help ease your pain and suffering, save you time, and ultimately move you closer to the life that you truly want to live with the time that he has on this wonderful planet.

I believe that we can live in alignment with who we truly are if we use our adversity to thrust ourselves toward the lives we desire instead of allowing it to hold us back. There are no secrets here. I will introduce to you some new concepts and help you gain a higher level of self-awareness—quite possibly the most underused resource we have. I hope to make you laugh through my own unbelievable stupidity. You'll certainly regain some hope in yourself. And, if you put in the work, you'll have the momentum you need to begin taking steps toward the life you've wanted to live for so long but have been either too afraid or too caught up in a destructive routine to experience.

The chapters are laid out in a way that will allow you to begin taking meaningful steps toward the life that you desire. To do that, I've included the absolutely essential elements that will assist you in learning more about yourself, the reasons you do the things you do, and the ways you can shift your mindset and actions to create your life instead of falling victim to it. The book flows mostly chronologically but also strategically, in a way that I found most helpful on my journey. While it's not required, I recommend that you read it from start to finish.

Although my story and the elements of it are unique to me, the themes and lessons learned, which make up the chapters, are where the value will be gained. As you go through the book, you'll notice the contrast between two different characters: a late-teen and early-twenties Jake who thought he knew everything, who was defiant to all authority and believed his actions only affected him; and mid-twenties Jake, who has spent roughly the past six years working, like his life depended on it, to overcome a decade-long journey to rock bottom.

I fought hard to learn everything I could from my mistakes and experiences while never giving up hope that one day my life would be drastically different from what it was at its lowest point. That transition between those two completely different versions of myself is a journey I hope you'll take with me and also undergo in your own unique way, whether that means overcoming your own harsh adversity or just improving your already decent life. It's a journey that extends far beyond the pages of this book, but I believe this book will be a crucial element for you to turn things around in your own life or to help others do so.

I want to help you grow, evolve, mature, and learn, but most of all I want you to choose the life you deserve because, as you'll learn, everything begins with a choice. The shift from who you are now to who you're going to be at the end of this book and in the weeks, months, and years that follow is going to require every verb in that last sentence (growing, evolving, maturing, learning) and then some. It won't be easy work, but it will be worth more than I could ever accurately describe. Hell, this is your life, so I could never accurately express how valuable and important that hard work will be to you.

Your future and everything you've ever dreamt of depend on you taking control of your life. Do the hard work. Reflect truthfully. Respect and love yourself enough to know that you deserve to be happy, fulfilled, and free from your current suffering or from that of your past. Shift your mindset so that living your life fully is no longer just a dream and is instead your reality. Climb out of rock bottom, whatever it is you're going through. Start using what you already know and will continue to learn to create a solid foundation that all your future endeavors can be built upon.

When we hear another person's story and relate to parts of it, we can say, "Hey, I'm not the only one." It's in that phrase that we then regain a bit of hope. That hope allows us to take a step out of the undesirable parts of our lives and into those that we've always longed for. Throughout this book, remember that this is my story. I'm a person who has lived these events, and I know how you feel. Fortunately, I've also made it past them, and I know how that feels as well. I want nothing more than for you to experience that same freedom I have found in overcoming adversity.

It's time you plant your feet firmly on solid ground and take your first steps toward a better life. If it wasn't hard, it wouldn't be worth it. If it wasn't worth it, you wouldn't do it. If you don't do it, you'll continue along the path you've been on until there is no time left. Choose a life that matters.

"The first step to getting somewhere is to decide that you are not going to stay where you are."

Unknown

1

SOMETIMES THE JOURNEY (TO ROCK BOTTOM) STARTS LONG BEFORE WE REALIZE

It takes a lot of reflection and self-analysis to truly understand how we arrived at a certain point in life. We can look back in time, pick apart the choices we made and the ones we didn't, and ponder how it might have turned out differently or how we can make better ones going forward.

I was twenty-one and lost. I sat on my green leather couch—still, emotionless, burnt out from roughly a year of daily blackouts and getting high to numb my gradually increasing emotional pain. In a room where the noise of cars whizzing by could usually be heard, I heard nothing but the subtle beating of my heart. A shell of myself sat on the couch, but the real me, the me I aspired to be, hovered above, looking down in disappointment at the unraveling of my life over the past year.

The me I aspired to be wanted answers. He wanted to know how his life had become such a seemingly unrecoverable mess. In years past, I had been like a perfect, untouched ball of yarn, full of potential and possibilities, but now I was a tangled mess that had experienced the skilled destruction of a curious cat with untrimmed claws and an abundance of energy. The cat had grabbed the ball of yarn somewhere in the middle and begun pulling, biting, and clawing until the yarn appeared useless and the only thing left to do was toss it out. Luckily, that wasn't true. Another option did exist. I could become useful again, but only after devoting an unknowable amount of time and patience into untangling the utter mess that I was.

It was that reflection, for the first time in nearly a year, and the colorful imagination of a ball of yarn that transported me back to seventh grade—a time when I was still a pristine, untouched ball of yarn. Okay, enough with the yarn metaphor, eh?

◘

I was fourteen, and my first year of middle school had quickly come to an end. I walked down the hall, opened my locker, and grabbed everything in it. I turned around, walked a few feet away, and chucked all but a few mostly unused notebooks into the trash can. I closed my locker for the last time as a seventh grader and made my way outside to wait for my mom to pick me up.

I had met dozens of people throughout the year, and my summer would mostly be consumed by hanging out with those new (and old) friends, interspersed with weekend visits to go see my dad. The first few weeks of summer had already passed by in a blur of bike riding, playing outside, and late nights.

I sometimes skipped those visits to my dad's house to stay with my friends, but this upcoming weekend was one I was looking forward to. We were going camping with some family friends, and I always looked forward to spending all day on the lake—fishing, water tubing, relaxing by the campfire, roasting marshmallows, and eavesdropping on cool adult conversations.

My mom arrived to pick me up in front of the school, and I waved bye to the few friends who remained waiting to be picked up. When we arrived home, I went upstairs to put my bag together and then went outside to shoot hoops until my dad arrived. Twenty minutes later, I heard the rumble of my dad's truck as he turned onto the road in front of my mom's house. I rolled the ball into the garage and ran toward the side door, pushing the button on the wall to close the garage. I ran to pick up my bag before peeking my head in the house. "Goodbye, Mom. I love you," I said, and excitedly ran toward my dad's vehicle. He rolled onto the cement slab I had just been shooting hoops on, and I climbed into the passenger seat.

"Hey, bud, how're you?" my dad asked.

"I'm doing well. Excited for the weekend!" I said, buckling my seatbelt.

"Me too! We're going to run home to get the camper, and then we're heading right out to the campsite. Derek and a few other people are already there."

"Sounds great," I said.

We drove through the alley and took a right. Thirty minutes later, we arrived at my dad's house. I hopped out of his truck and ran inside to grab a package of my favorite fruit snacks, which he always kept in the pantry. My dad backed his truck up to the camper. I went back outside to lower the camper onto the hitch. My dad finished hooking it up, and after gathering some last-minute supplies, we pulled out of the driveway to head toward the campsite.

When we arrived, my dad maneuvered his vehicle so that he could slowly back the camper into our designated spot. His friend, Derek, guided us with one-handed motions toward his body, holding a blue and silver can of Busch Light in his other hand. The brakes gave a quick squeak as my dad stopped and put the vehicle into park.

My feet were on the ground the second my dad let go of the shifting lever. We began setting up our home for the next few days. This was a newer camper that we had only used once or twice before, and I was looking forward to having a real mattress to sleep on instead of the unbearable air mattress I had come to know so well.

After an hour, we were set up and ready to sit down by the fire. My brother Ryan and his girlfriend would be arriving later, after he got done with work. I was excited to spend the weekend with everyone and stay up late under the starry night sky cooking marshmallows and pudgie pies.

If you're not familiar with a pudgie pie, you're missing out. You take two separate square iron pans, each at the end of a long metal rod, and tuck a piece of bread into each pan and pile your favorite fillings inside. Then, you bring the two pans together to form a container-like contraption and hold it over the fire to cook it. Voilà! That's Pudgie Pie 101.

Derek and I had always joked that we were going to open our own pudgie pie business, so it had become our tradition anytime we went camping to indulge in the goodness of a pizza, apple, cherry, or any other random variety of pudgie pie sandwich we could cook up with the supplies we had on hand.

It was early in the evening by the time we sat down around the fire, so we began making dinner. My brother and his girlfriend arrived just as we had finished cooking. There were about fifteen of us now, and the night was just getting started.

Darkness began to blanket the sky, and as it slowly settled on our campsites, a noticeable intoxication came over the people in the surrounding area. A mixture of music, laughing, and mumbled conversations could be heard from all sides.

I stared into the fire and its hypnotizing dance of flames and pulsing, red-hot coals. I ate my dinner and enjoyed feeling the fire's warmth against my legs. Dessert was a couple of carefully roasted marshmallows. I sat, patiently watching my marshmallow turn golden brown from the painfully slow process of roasting. If you've ever roasted a marshmallow, you know that the task of roasting it and keeping it on the stick isn't always successful, but it's always worth it. I noticed the fire warming my face as I looked up, waiting for my eyes to adjust to the newfound darkness that enveloped the immediate areas just outside the glow.

When my eyes adjusted, a blue drink being plucked from the cooler caught my attention. I was and still am a sucker for anything blue-raspberry flavored, so, naturally, I had to ask what it tasted like. "Hey Tonya, what is that?" I said curiously, but innocently, as if only to receive a response and nothing more.

"It's Boone's Farm," she said, turning the bottle to reveal the flavor spelled out on the label. "Blue Hawaiian. It's similar to a wine cooler. Do you want to try it?" she continued.

"Errmm, I don't know . . ." I replied while inquisitively looking in my dad's direction. The blue drink just looked so good. I had tried a sip of beer before this instance and thought it was disgusting, so a little sip of a wine cooler couldn't hurt anything.

"Go ahead," my dad said.

The cup was filled about half full, and the liquid was joined by a few ice cubes. I looked down into it as I swirled the drink around inside. I smelled it, intentionally procrastinating as if I were too nervous to give it a taste in front of the real and legal, alcohol-consuming adults surrounding me. Eventually I tipped it back and let the fruity drink splash into my mouth. The slight taste of alcohol made me wince a bit, but that was soon overpowered by its overall sweetness.

"How was it?" someone on the other side of the fire asked.

"It's good. I like it," I replied a few seconds later. Chuckles ensued as I took another drink. For the next thirty minutes, our night carried on like normal, without much attention to the red cup in my hand.

I tipped the cup back, drinking the last few drops. The ice cubes slid onto my lips, making a noise as they ricocheted against the plastic cup. I set the cup on the picnic table next to me and looked at Tonya. "Oh, wow. That was good." Again, laughter arose from several people around the fire.

"You want some more?" she asked. Again, I looked in my dad's general direction and said, "Errmm, well . . . I don't know."

My dad said, "Fine, but just one more, and that's it." I jumped up from my seat and walked over to the cooler to drop some ice chunks into my cup. I tipped the bottle upside down, pouring the blue good-ness into my glass until it was full.

I put the half-full bottle back into the cooler and quietly returned to my seat with my drink. I drank it casually, like the adults around me, for the next hour. The more I drank, the better it tasted. It also didn't hurt that I was motivated by the "cool factor" of hanging out with the adults and the occasional laughter from something I said or did, which was likely encouraged by my mild intoxication.

I was feeling a warming sensation in my head, cheeks, and extrem-ities. Naturally, I had to slow my speech so that I could talk clearly and maintain the appearance that I was sober. I had begun to feel, for the first time, the effects of the alcohol blanketing my normal personality and demeanor.

"How're you feeling, Jake?" my brother asked from across the fire.

"I feel fine. A little different, but I'm good. I kind of like it. I feel relaxed," I said, awkwardly trying to describe the foreign feelings of early intoxication.

Someone stood up to grab a beer from the cooler and asked if I wanted one. I was hesitant, as I remembered what my dad had said just an hour ago. I could feel the alcohol warming my face as I pon-dered the question. My innate curiosity wanted me to answer yes. I wanted to know what would happen and how I would feel if I kept drinking. Although I had tried beer before, I wondered what this beer tasted like. But my respect for my dad wanted me to answer no so that he wasn't put in the difficult position of saying no for me.

I remained silent, acting as if I hadn't heard the person who asked me if I wanted a beer. The longer I sat there, the more intensely I be-gan to feel the effects of the alcohol I had recently drunk.

My moderately impaired speech and off-key actions had become entertainment among those whom I was camping with. The feeling I received from making everyone laugh, being the center of attention, was great. I may have been apprehensive to continue drinking, but the attention I received from my family and friends was the fuel I craved, enticing me to keep drinking. Sure, I might upset my dad or put him in an awkward position, but it was one night. What could it hurt? Besides, it appeared as though the more I drank and acted out, the more everyone enjoyed themselves.

At this point, I think everyone had had enough to drink that I was able to get away with more than I usually would have. I was feeling goofy and relaxed, and I didn't want those feelings or the joy I got out of entertaining everyone to end. Emboldened by a couple cups of Boone's Farm, I began pouring drinks as I wanted them, with or without my dad's approval. "Want a shot?" someone asked. I obliged them by tipping back the small plastic shot glass I was handed. I cringed as the strong and unfamiliar taste puckered my face and burned as it went down.

All-out laughter emanated throughout our campsite as my intoxication evolved into tirades about random topics or people. Their laughter, my ultimate motivator, was the fuel that drove me to keep drinking, regardless of the consequences.

The night continued along with me finishing more than just the one bottle I had first sampled from. My intoxicated entertainment went from innocent and harmless to a point of all-out belligerence. I was cursing, struggling to stand up, and close to blacking out.

My brother came over to help me to my feet and said, "Jake, let's go for a walk." Instinctively, I closed one eye and squinted the other that remained open to focus on the man holding me up.

"Ryan?" the words slurred from my mouth, louder than necessary.

"Yes, it's me, Jake. Let's go for a walk," he said as he helped me to my feet. I kept one eye shut and the other half open while looking at my feet in order to maintain some ability while walking—my brother did most of the stabilizing for me.

We made our way past the picnic table I'd been sitting on toward the paved road behind me. "Are you doing all right?" Ryan asked.

"I'ma doin' fiiine . . ." I mumbled back.

"Jake, you know you cannot tell Mom about this. You know that, right?"

"Yah, yeahhh, yeeah. I knooow."

"Seriously, Jake," my brother said, trying to confirm my compliance.

"Ryan, I'm n-nnot going to s-ss-ay a thing," I said, leaning into him.

"Are you going to remember this in the morning?" Ryan asked in a concerned manner.

"Well . . . I don't know. I've nevvverr been drrrunk before," I replied in the same smart-ass tone I had been using to crack jokes around the fire.

"All right, well, let's head back to the fire. I think you should go to bed soon."

"Yeah, I willinna little bit."

We turned around and made it back to my spot by the fire. My night continued for another hour as I relished laughs at my amusing drunkenness. I was done drinking at this point, but the alcohol I had guzzled over the past few hours was enough to carry me through the rest of the evening.

When things began to wind down and I'd had enough of the fun, I called it a night and asked for help getting into the camper and into bed. My dad walked me to my bed in the camper, laid me down, and covered me up.

"Good night, Jake. I love you. See you in the morning." I was mostly asleep before he finished his words.

When the morning came, I was rudely awoken by the foul smell of a blanket soaked in alcohol and scattered with hotdogs and hamburger meat, which I'd vomited up in my sleep from dinner the previous night. I proceeded to get up carefully so as not to make a mess of the puke and folded the blanket over to contain it. I laid it next to the camper as I walked outside to a new morning.

I was feeling like a champ, so I began cooking breakfast. I cracked and fried the eggs, cooked the bacon over the fire, and made toast in the various toasters around our campsite. I finished cooking my morning buffet just as the majority of my fellow "drinking buddies" from the night prior were waking up. They, however, were feeling slightly more hungover than I was—a term that I had heard but of which I knew nothing. Years later, hangovers became real for me, but for now they were only visible in the attitudes and actions of those around me.

I didn't know how to handle being sober in the presence of the people I had gotten wasted in front of only a few hours ago. It was the first time I had been drunk, and it had been far outside the expectations anyone had when the weekend began. Nevertheless, it had happened, and I was fine now. There were no consequences, so what was there to worry about?

It's one thing to wake up the morning after a night of drinking to sit around with friends and attempt to recall a night of drunkenness by piecing together snapshots from each person's recollection. It's a completely different thing when you have to piece together the night before with stories from adults you admire while eating breakfast around the remains of the fire where it all occurred. It's easy, as I would find out years later, to laugh and joke about the drunken antics of yourself and your group of friends. However, it's not as easy to have to recall your belligerence through stories being told to you by the very people you were cursing out and calling names the evening prior.

In the moment, I felt compelled to laugh and act as though I was still the confident, tough guy they'd experienced when I was drunk, keeping inside of me the true confusion I felt about the whole evening and my choices within it. If not for the alcohol, I never would've acted out in such a way. Alcohol made that version of myself come alive, and it was now up to me to decide what to do with the cringe-worthy stories being told to me from the night before.

The rest of the weekend went on as I had initially expected, alcohol free, and consisting of fishing, jet-skiing, and genuine conversation with family and friends.

When the weekend came to an end, we all began packing up our campsite, and by noon on Sunday we were pulling onto the road to head for home. The ride home was no different than any other ride with my dad. The one thing that stands out now is that I don't recall talking about that night of drunkenness with my dad on the way back home, or ever. Maybe it was as hard for him to talk about as it was for me to hear those stories the next day. Maybe it wasn't something that warranted discussion, because he and I both knew it was a one-time thing. Maybe it really didn't need to be talked about because, all things considered, it was a mostly harmless incident. I can't be fully certain why nothing was said, just as I can't be sure it would've done any good against the powerful forces that would guide me down the path I chose years later.

"Are you coming to my game this Tuesday?" I asked my dad.

"I'll be there. I can't wait," he said. "We're going to go home and unload the camper and then I'll take you back to your mom's house later this afternoon, sound okay?"

"Sounds great!" I replied.

I returned to my mom's house later that evening, and upon walking in the door, one memory could not be silenced: the conversation I'd had with my brother. *Jake, you know you cannot tell Mom about this* rang through my head repeatedly.

I didn't have any secrets to keep from my mom. The worst lies I remember telling her prior to this were the occasional exaggerations about how well I did on a math test or a stretch of the truth when I got in trouble at school. I was a genuine mama's boy and a well-mannered, hardworking kid who knew right from wrong.

Now, at age fourteen, I had to carry the burden of keeping this one drunken night a secret indefinitely. There aren't any written rules about how long it's necessary to keep secrets until you can safely tell them, but this one seemed like something that should remain a secret for a long time.

I carried that secret with me into a new school year. It began as, at most, a slight nudge from the path I was on, but it would amplify into a new way to bond with friends who were just as curious about drinking as I was upon seeing that bright blue drink being pulled from the cooler.

"Don't feel sorry
for yourself
if you have chosen
the wrong road,
turn around."

Edgar Cayce

2

THERE'S A FIRST TIME
FOR EVERYTHING

The eighth-grade school year was underway, and—aside from the fact that I had gotten drunk for the first time—I'd had a routine summer, hanging out with friends and playing sports, that had whizzed by. During study hall, a few friends and I found ourselves sharing the stories of our summers. I brought up the night I went camping with my family.

"No way. So did I, man!" Rick responded. "Dude, I got so drunk with my family when we went fishing over the summer," he whispered.

Andrew listened intently, his interest piqued, and then asked what it was like to be drunk.

"I don't know how to explain it, really," Rick said, and I agreed. "We should get a few people together one of these weekends and get drunk." We gathered up our stuff and discussed who we could invite. Rick threw out a few names of people he had drunk with a few times over the summer.

"Cool, well, let's see if they want to, then we'll find a weekend we're all free and get together somewhere," I said, as a self-proclaimed cofounder of this brilliant idea we had come up with in our forty-five-minute study hall.

We stood up and went our separate ways to our next class. Throughout the rest of that year and those that followed, we found ways to make our plan come to fruition. Just as we had discussed, the three of us, along with a few other friends, became regular drinking buddies, gathering on occasional weekends throughout that first year. The frequency with which we gathered increased as the years went on.

□

It was the summer after ninth grade, and I was going to get my driver's license and become one of the youngest kids in my class to have a car. Getting a driver's license is one of those monumental life events that make you feel like you're one step closer to be becoming a bona fide adult member of society. It's another step into greater responsibility.

Sophomore year brought more of what every school year does: a scheduled routine throughout the week and a release of pent-up, teenage energy at the end of it. For me, high school consisted of working a part-time job, playing video games, spending time with family and friends, and regularly planned weekends of binge drinking.

What started out as a friendly study hall discussion had transitioned into what most reasonable people would consider concerning, especially for teenage kids. However, we were just getting started and gave no sign of looking back or ceasing our drinking routine. Aside from an occasional weekend of playing cards or video games with other friends, our drinking crew was always willing to gather.

A CRACK IN THE DAM

"You want to go out to Stratford this weekend?" I asked Andrew as we walked down the hallway to our next class.

"Yeah, what's going on out there?" he responded.

"This girl I know is throwing a party while her mom is out of town."

"Yeah, I'm definitely in. We'll talk about it more later," Andrew said before turning into his classroom while I continued on down the hall to mine.

We got out of our last class of the day and met up in the hallway to hash out the details for the night. "I'll see you at six!" I said as I slammed my locker and flung my backpack over my shoulder.

I continued on my way out of the high school and into my car to go home and relax for a few hours before going to pick up Andrew. I texted him shortly before six o'clock. "Yo, I'll be there in 15," I typed out and sent before I pulled out of my driveway.

"Good deal," he replied.

I parked and walked up to the door to go into the house. Andrew's dad, Alan, was there to open the door and greet me. We caught up a bit while Andrew and I joked around with him.

"What're you going to do tonight, Pops?" Andrew asked his dad.

"I think Karen and I are going to go grab some dinner and then come back here and watch a movie. You guys be safe and have a good night. Will you be coming back tonight?" Andrew and I looked at each other, both honestly unsure, and filled in the blanks of each other's sentences.

"Umm, I'm not quite sure where we're staying yet . . ." I said.

"Yeah, I think we may stay out in Stratford, but we're not sure," Andrew added.

"I'm sure we could stay at my dad's house if we wanted to as well," I told Alan.

"Okay, well, I'll see you later, or tomorrow, maybe. Have fun," Alan said as we slipped on our shoes, unaware of the real plans Andrew and I had for the evening.

"Thanks, Pops. Catch you later," Andrew said as we closed the door.

"Good seeing you, Alan," I shouted through the door as it closed behind us.

Over the years, the initial lie I had told my mom about my weekend camping trip had ballooned into a web of lies. I added another new strand to it nearly every weekend. My life had become a two-pronged reality: one of appearing to live my life according to some societally acceptable version of a high-school-aged kid, and another of covering up my tracks with creative lies with collaboration from my friends to keep our weekend rituals alive.

This weekend, much like many others, began with plans of going to a party I had been invited to by a group of friends from a different school twenty minutes away. We pulled up to the house where the party was. Five or six vehicles had already parked on the road. I parked my little, teal Pontiac Grand Am behind one of the big trucks. Andrew and I got out of the car, and I grabbed the bottle of vodka discretely wrapped in a sweatshirt and hidden under my spare tire in the trunk.

"Greg! What's up, man? How've you been?" I yelled out to a friend who was talking and smoking a cigarette in the garage.

"Jake! Not a whole lot, man. Ready to get drunk, that's for sure," he said, laughing and exhaling the smoke from his cigarette into the air.

"I hear you, man. Well, we're going to go inside. We'll catch up later!"

"Sounds good!" he said as he turned around.

Over the next hour, I introduced Andrew to a few people I knew he would like, and we began mixing drinks in our Gatorade bottles. By the time I had introduced Andrew to half a dozen or so people, we had both drunk enough to not really care about the formal introductions. We were comfortable just roaming around, catching up with friends, and meeting new people. We regrouped every little bit to gauge our drunkenness and chat with mutual friends.

"There are a lot of people here now," I said as I pulled out my phone to check the time. I looked to my left toward Andrew, who was blankly staring off across the room at the faux wood walls. The numbers on my phone read 11:54 in white light. We had been there for several hours, and both of us had had enough to drink. Our mutual tiredness carried us to the nearby couches in the living room, where our mutual drunkenness settled in further.

"Duuude . . . I'm drrrunnk," Andrew said, leaning back into the '90s-style couch he was sitting on.

"Oh man, I know. Same here," I replied with my head tilted back, resting on the top of the couch's backrest. With no evidence that the party would be dying down soon, I tapped Andrew's knee. "Come on, get up. Let's go wander around."

"Ughh, man. All right." We casually made our way around the house and outside for the next hour, chatting with people and nursing our drinks.

I finished off the little bit that was in my bottle and then tossed it into the trash can inside the entryway. I leaned into Andrew. "I feel slightly less drunk than before, but I'm ready to find a place to crash," I said, loud enough for him to hear me over the music.

"Yeah, it seems things have died down in here. I think I'm going to try crashing on the couch," Andrew said, with one eye trying to focus on me and the other apparently already attempting to fall asleep.

"I'm going to find Kelly and see if it's okay that we crash here," I said as Andrew staggered toward the living room. Kelly was the host, and I supposed it would have been wise of me to clear our sleeping over before we got drunk and became incapable of driving, but that wasn't the case.

I found her in the mix of a group of four or five other people. "Kelly, Andrew and I are so ready to pass out. Are you okay with us finding a place to crash here?"

"Yeah, that's fine. It's just going to be hard, because it's already a pretty full house," she said in a manner that led me to believe it was only okay if we really, truly needed a place to crash.

If there's anything I hate, it's being a burden. I have a keen sense of awareness when it comes to deciphering the true intent disguised behind people's words. I don't know where it comes from, but that emotional intelligence is what helps me relate to people so well. In this instance, to know that the "yes" I had received also came with an un-communicated "but." As in, "Yes, it's okay, but it'd be best if you stayed somewhere else . . ."

I walked away disappointed. I didn't feel comfortable staying over-night. "Andrew, are you awake?" I said in a raised voice. I grasped his shoulder and shook him until I felt he was alert enough to understand and respond to what I was saying.

"Ugghhhh, whaaaat?" he said with eyes shut.

"Would you be okay with driving back to your dad's house?"

"Dude, it's like one in the morning, and we're still drunk."

"I know, but Kelly said it's full and she needs the space for people who already asked to sleep over," I said, half lying about her words but conveying what I believed she meant.

"Jake, dude. Screw her. I'm sleeping here," he insisted with eyes still closed.

I sat down in the same spot I was in roughly an hour before. I began talking with a few people sitting around me about their night. After a few minutes, someone I barely knew interrupted: "Hey, are you guys getting up soon? I'm sleeping there."

"I suppose, if you've claimed it," I said to him as I leaned forward to stand up. "Andrew, come on, man. We're not staying here."

"Ugh, fine," he said, rolling over and standing up.

We walked out to the entry area to put our shoes on and opened the door to walk out into the cool summer night. The hairs on my arms stood up, in part because of the chill but mostly because I was unsettled that I was about to get into my car and drive roughly fifteen miles back to Andrew's dad's house.

"Later, guys. See you again soon," I said to the group of familiar faces outside smoking their last cigarette of the night.

"You guys are leaving?" they said.

"Yeah, nowhere to sleep, so we're heading out," I replied.

"All right, be safe and see you soon!" they said.

We walked down the heavily worn, blacktopped driveway with a noticeably impaired stride. The orange glow of the streetlights fell softly onto the cars parked on the road. My car lay just outside the streetlight's reach. I hoped this would limit the visibility of Andrew and me making our way to my car. Then again, I was hoping for a lot during this moment in time. I walked across the street with my head looking left, right, left, right—scanning for cops or any snoopy neighbors who might be waiting to turn us in. *Act natural,* I told myself. We were in a tiny little farm town, but my fears of getting caught were as real as any fear I had ever felt before.

I inserted the key into my door and twisted my hand to the left until the car was unlocked. With a lift on the door handle, I pulled the door open and sat down in my seat. I pushed the unlock button so that Andrew could get in.

"Well, I'm not tired anymore," I said, looking at Andrew, who was sitting in the passenger seat to my right.

"Me either, man. Let's get this over with," he said with an invigorated sense of confidence.

I looked around one last time to scan the area for anything that might pose a concern in terms of us getting caught. All clear!

For the next fifteen miles, I was more present and in tune with my driving than ever before in my life. I transitioned between checking my speed, looking in my rearview mirror, turning my brights off as cars approached, keeping my vehicle about a foot from the center line, and maintaining that distance the entire drive home. It became a continuous cycle to ensure not only that I got us home safe but also that we didn't end the night in jail.

I was more nervous than ever before in my life, and rightfully so, but I felt that I was driving well. I set my cruise at fifty-eight when the speed limit was fifty-five. I was doing a good job maintaining speed and keeping my vehicle straight. My hands gripped the steering wheel tightly at ten and two—a lesson I had learned in the not-too-distant driver's education class I had gone through.

"Are you doing all right, man?" Andrew asked.

"Yeah man, I'm doing good. This was really dumb to do, but I'm fine," I said without taking my eyes off of the road.

Roughly twenty minutes later, we had made it back to Andrew's dad's house and pulled into the driveway safely. We made food and passed out.

I woke up the following morning around ten. The bright, late-morning sun was shining through the basement windows. I gathered my keys and phone and went upstairs to put my shoes on before heading out the door. I drove home and went about the rest of my weekend like any other sixteen-year-old kid.

In the wake of what I had just done no more than eight hours prior, I was unaffected. I was emotionless about it. I undoubtedly knew it wasn't the right thing to do, but I don't remember feeling the slightest bit of remorse or guilt. The reality was that I had just gotten away with something profoundly dangerous and stupid, and I had woken up the next morning without having to pay any apparent consequences for my actions.

That lone fact would help to keep me on the path I was becoming all too comfortable with. It may have begun out of a random study hall conversation in eighth grade and soon after transitioned into getting drunk with friends on the weekend, but at this point it had evolved into the first major step down the wrong path.

Fortunately, I can say we made it home without a single mishap on our journey that night. Unfortunately, the rush I'd felt, as well as the fact that I had come nowhere near getting caught, would make this far from the last time I drove drunk. Hindsight tells me that this was simply the next step down the grim path I had recently committed to.

It was like the first time I had gotten drunk—how the circumstances came together to allow it to happen without major repercussions, and it began a slow unraveling of my life. This night of escaping the consequences only emboldened me. Every time I chose to do it again in the future and got away with it, my ego would inflate a little more, providing a sense of invincibility.

The fear that motivated me to be aware of the smallest details on that first night slowly eroded until I drove drunk nearly every time I drank. That first time I got behind the wheel was a crack in the dam that began letting the smallest amount of water drip through.

Slowly, those choices began wearing away the dam. My morals, values, and everything else that held my life together would soon erode until there was nothing left but memories of what once was and, once again, a powerful river.

"Unhappiness
is not knowing
what we want
and killing ourselves
to get it."

———————

Don Herold

3

PLAN OR FAIL.
THERE IS NO IN-BETWEEN.

As I've gained more life experience through my years, I've learned that I could've often saved myself some hardship if I would've only listened to my friends and family who had my best interests in mind. However, discerning which advice was and was not in my best interest was a whole other challenge altogether.

There are endless examples I could recite, but the moral of it all is this: you need to have a level of awareness about yourself and what you want your life to look like in order for it to come together as you dream, hope, or desire it to. In other words, you need to plan how you want your future to look, or it will simply fall in line according to the random choices you make on a daily basis.

I pseudo-planned my future through my junior and senior years of high school, thinking about colleges I wanted to attend. Much like the vast majority of high school seniors, I had no idea what I wanted to do for the rest of my life, but I figured submitting some college applications wasn't the worst choice. I knew that I wasn't willing to take on tens of thousands of dollars in student loan debt while drudging my way toward a degree I wasn't certain about, but I also wasn't going to ask or expect my parents to pay my way through it either. I took it upon myself, with the extra incentive of a favorable enlistment bonus, to join the Army Reserves.

After I had officially enlisted, I went about the remainder of my senior year as normal—school, partying most weekends, and doing enough work to pass with a B or C. I graduated in the summer of 2009, a few weeks before leaving to attend basic training and my military job training in finance.

I came back after roughly four months of military training, completed a semester of school at the University of Wisconsin–Stevens Point, and then headed to Fort McCoy, Wisconsin, to conduct premobilization training for my deployment to Kuwait. I had volunteered for this deployment because I had made good friends with a guy who was already going on the deployment, and I'd rather deploy with him to a generally safe location than deploy in the next year or two with people I didn't have a relationship with, to an unknown and probably less safe location like Iraq or Afghanistan.

Over the summer of 2010, we completed our training. It was during that time that I first faced a consequence for my actions. After graduating high school, I had taken a liking to the sensation that follows from smoking a certain leafy, pungent plant. I continued smoking weed throughout the summer that surrounded my predeployment training.

Little did I know that the military tests for drug use—and quite often. I couldn't drink enough water, exercise enough, or take enough niacin to pass a drug screen. The amount of THC in my body wasn't something that could be diluted in the few hours we were given to provide a urine sample. I walked out of the bathroom in our barracks, cup held above my head with the most transparent liquid I had ever seen. It was clearer than the eight or nine bottles of water I had drunk throughout the past hour, something I didn't know was possible. However, I was confident that, in a lab, its chemical makeup would prove to contain much more than just H_2O.

About a week later, they confirmed that I had failed, and I was faced with potentially being kicked off of the deployment. Luckily, after much disciplinary protocol and many meetings with my unit leadership and the military police, I was able to go on the deployment. Somehow, my leadership saw something in me that I, being the jackass that I was, failed to see in myself.

During the deployment, I became slightly less of a jackass, but I was still just as defiant to the ritualistic and standard conduct expected of all military members, especially us in the lower ranks. I came home from that deployment a year later with what was likely more money than all of my broke college friends combined. I had a few goals—one of which was to create an indie T-shirt company, another to reenroll into college—but first, I was determined to make up for lost time with friends who had been, as I had seen on social media, living the life. Once I returned home, I would be able to enjoy the life that every college-aged kid dreams of: all-nighters, hooking up with hot chicks, hanging with your bros, indulging in the era of YOLO, and experimenting with, well, whatever was offered. I've since learned that nearly every bit of that is entirely fruitless and unrewarding when compared with the pursuit of lasting achievement and impact, but that's an entire book in itself.

I had just turned twenty-one, and I proceeded to try to find joy and fulfillment in each and every one of those activities previously mentioned. No more than a few hours after returning home and hugging my family, I was smoking the bowl of weed my friends had ceremoniously packed for my return. After that, it was off to the bars to begin the process of making up for lost time.

It was that same motivator that led me and the friends I was deployed with to book a trip to Las Vegas shortly before leaving Kuwait. Less than a month after coming home, a friend I was deployed with, Ben, and I got into his car and drove from central Wisconsin to Las Vegas—roughly a day-and-a-half drive to the west. He was moving to Las Vegas to literally "try his hand" at a professional poker career. I couldn't help but think that a day or two's worth of driving would provide some unforgettable experiences, so I offered to go with. I also knew that getting more than half an ounce of weed onto an airplane would prove difficult, and sneaking it into my luggage in the backseat of his car was a much better option.

I'll spare you the mundane repetition of replaying every day I was in Vegas, which consisted of—you guessed it—drinking large quantities of alcohol, attempting to light up the dance floor at clubs, losing some money gambling, blacking out, and smoking lots of weed to help reduce the miserable hangovers that followed drinking until five in the morning for over a week straight. I somehow stayed out of trouble, but did manage to spend just over ten thousand dollars in the eleven days I remained in Vegas.

I took a single second to audit my actions while I was in Vegas, and my severely wounded bank accounts signaled that it was time to go home. I sat down at a guest computer in the lobby of a casino, transferred over some of the money I had saved while on deployment to my checking account, and booked my flight home. I did so knowing this trip had gone far off the rails, but I figured I'd be able to guide my life back toward a semblance of normalcy once I returned home and officially moved into the apartment I had arranged with my friend Rick. Yes, the same Rick I sat in study hall with eighth grade year, planning our weekend binge drinking.

I flew into the small airport outside my hometown in central Wisconsin. Rick picked me up, and we made our way to the apartment, my new home. Over the next week, I moved my stuff in and continued on with habits I had created for myself: blacking out from alcohol every day, smoking weed, and taking "uppers" or "speed"—ADHD medication like Adderall, Ritalin, and Vyvanse—so that I had motivation and energy to get out of the house. I justified all of this as a way to deal with the misery my life was becoming—or, more honestly, had already become.

During the months that followed my return home from deployment and Las Vegas, my life continued to spiral out of control. I'm going to skip over most of the details pertaining to the physical and mental state I was in at this point because they will be addressed in more detail later in the book. For now, just know that I was lost and relying on heavy doses of alcohol and drugs to simply make it through each day.

Before returning home, I'd assumed that I would be able to seamlessly transition back into civilian life and that things would continue as they were roughly a year prior. Unfortunately, what soldiers often fail to realize—and what causes them trouble as they transition back into civilian life—is that the life they left is rarely the life they return to. The differences between a pre-deployment and post-deployment home, whether you're literally living in the same house or are simply back on American soil, are subtle yet often paralyzing. My greatest challenges were no longer being able to authentically connect with my civilian friends who had gone about living their lives over the past year and being separated from my military friends by hundreds of miles. These challenges, coupled with two months of nonstop drinking behind me, made the journey ahead difficult.

I had fallen so far from the path I had laid out for myself before returning home that I no longer acted in accordance with the dreams that once driven me, and was only motivated by getting my next high so that I could dull my pain. If I needed groceries, booze, or weed, I never hesitated to hop in my car, no matter how intoxicated I was. My life felt like it was happening *to* me, rather than being controlled *by* me. Maybe that's my way of dissociating myself from a part of my life I'm not proud of, even if I have become grateful for it. Time and time again, I disregarded the warnings in their various forms: being followed by cops, disappointing my family and myself, watching my bank accounts drain in exchange for alcohol and baggies of weed. Maybe it was that my fear had become so negligible over the years and my ego so inflated that they no longer warranted a response to the close calls and continual disappointment.

The word decision, as in the decision to do or not do something, is a vitally important one. Whether we like it or not, it's our choices that create our life, and 99 percent of the time, we're in control of them. As we grow older, we're gradually given more responsibility and freedom to act on our own within society. Although it feels great to reach those new points of responsibility, I believe it also leads to one of the greatest challenges of reaching adulthood: being entrusted by our fellow humans to make the right decisions while we're still figuring out some of life's most monumental challenges as we go along.

I, like you probably did, found myself dealing with the newfound responsibilities of being a twenty-one-year-old adult. I was in an apartment on my own and fully free to live life as I desired. The irony of it all is that I wasn't living the life I desired. I was living a life that I was choosing, but it felt more like I was reacting to my life rather than consciously and intentionally choosing it. That's where reflection comes in. If anything, I hope this book serves to interrupt your daily routine. I hope these words that you're reading right now force you to stop and think about the life you're living and how the choices you're making are creating it. Then, decide if you're hitting the benchmarks along the path to where you want to be, and adjust your choices based off of that.

WHEN LIFE BEGINS TO UNRAVEL

Remove yourself from my story for a minute. Don't say, "Well, that element of Jake's story doesn't apply to my life, so there's nothing I can take from it." Take a few moments to think about all of the milestones you have already reached or will reach someday. Will you be graduating high school, going to college, getting your first serious job, moving out on your own, taking dating seriously, turning twenty-one, paying bills, getting offered or trying drugs, experiencing the death of a close family member, taking care of a relative, or getting pregnant unexpectedly? Life often unloads a serious amount of responsibility onto us without ever hesitating to see what other issues we may already have going on. All of these responsibilities must remain in balance, and as we add more to our plate, it becomes more and more difficult. It's also important to realize that each individual responsibility carries its own specific weight or importance in relation to the others based on our own specific ambitions, values, and incredible uniqueness of our individual lives.

To make it more difficult, some of these newfound responsibilities often come with serious consequences if not managed appropriately. We have minimal experience in appropriately managing many of these often newfound responsibilities, so when one thing begins to fall out of balance—bills, grades, health, drinking responsibly, loss of a job, an unexpected death, or pregnancy—we have to work extra hard to balance our lives while still managing all the other preexisting responsibilities. Keeping our lives together is a never-ending process of trial and error.

No matter what your social media news feed tells you about how "together" your friends' lives are, it's simply not an accurate depiction of the truth. They're just as clueless as you are, floundering around behind their screen, asking themselves *WTF?* a lot and trying to figure it out as they go. We often vastly underestimate the immense benefit of sharing our stories, thoughts, experiences, and challenges openly with others. Keep that in the front of your mind. I promise it'll benefit you greatly to confide in others and not to compare yourself to those who appear to have it all together.

I've found that it's in those moments, when we're putting in the additional work to keep our lives in balance—or to keep them from falling further apart—that we're most vulnerable. A relationship may come to an end, we might come across some financial struggle; maybe we realize our friends don't have our best interests in mind, or possibly we've just returned home from a yearlong deployment. These incidents, which sometimes seem small in the grand scheme of things, can send us down a path that leads to undesirable spots emotionally, physically, and psychologically.

I'm sure you've had plenty of instances when you've found yourself in a situation in which something didn't feel right, so you left to avoid any potential trouble. But as easy as it may have been for you in that moment, being responsible and making better decisions isn't always that easy. On top of that, it's not always obvious that our choices are leading us down an undesirable path. Through the countless talks I've had with other people and my own personal experiences, I've learned that this is often how it begins—with one small, practically harmless choice that, when compounded with other barely measurable decisions, turns into something much more dangerous and hard to recover from.

That's exactly how I went from a teenager graduating high school, living a mostly average life, to an early twenty-something addicted to alcohol who got high and blackout drunk daily to numb the pain from the misery that his life had become.

> *"Actions and consequences are a packaged deal."*
> —Unknown

TIME'S UP

As I heavily reflected on my life prior to and during the writing of this book, I realized the importance of reflection, journaling, thinking, planning—whatever you want to call it. As I've moved past the version of myself you'll continue to read about in this book and met people at varying levels of the success ladder, I've found that every single person who aspires for more makes a daily ritual of journaling—writing down thoughts, reflecting on the day before, planning for the future, setting goals, making sense of feelings and emotions.

It was through that reflection that I was able to recall the event that led me closer to the edge of the cliff overlooking rock bottom. That reflection is what forced me to realize that every time I "successfully" drove drunk wasn't a badge of authority or trophy to admire but a warning sign that my luck would eventually run out. I had easily driven drunk "successfully" over four hundred times in my life, and I'd guess no fewer than one hundred times in the five months I had been home from my deployment. There were no signs that I would ever get caught, other than the basic fundamentals of society—that no one goes their entire life without eventually being dealt the consequences of their actions.

"Rick, what's up, man? How was work?" I said from the kitchen, feeling the cold January wind blow in with my roommate as he walked through the door.

"Not bad, man, but I'm glad it's Friday," he said while kneeling down to take off his boots.

"Yeah, definitely. Are we doing anything tonight?" I asked, certain that we would find something, but not sure of what yet.

"I'm not sure. I don't really feel like going out to the bars tonight, plus I saw that it's supposed to snow," he replied.

"Why don't we have some people over and drink here?" I offered up while stirring the food I was making on the stove.

"Yeah, that sounds great!" Rick replied.

We spent the next few hours texting and calling friends while cleaning up the house and running to the store to pick up alcohol. By eight o'clock, we had fifteen people in our house drinking, playing games, and listening to music. Over the next three or four hours, we all had enough to drink that driving should have been out of the question. However, someone introduced the brilliant idea of going out to the bars. Backed by support from the other intoxicated people, the popular vote was in, and we decided to leave the house and go out.

"Driver!" I called as I walked to the door to put my shoes on. Snow had begun to slowly fall and accumulate on the ground and vehicles outside. It was nothing to be alarmed by, at least not for people from Wisconsin, but just enough to approach the roads with a little extra caution; that is, in addition to the extra caution I was already taking while driving under the influence. Myself and three other friends loaded into my car to head to the bars, while two other cars loaded up and left our house to head to a bar called Green's. We stopped at a few bars, all of which were mostly dead because of the heavier snow coming down consistently now. We finished our drinks at a bar called Someplace Else and got back into my car to make our way toward the last stop of the night.

We made our way to Green's bar to reunite with the friends whom we had been drinking with earlier at our house. The wet snow crunched underneath my tires as I pulled into the parking lot. We unloaded from my car, had a few drinks, and within an hour were loading back up to drive the two miles home.

I pulled safely into my driveway and reached to put my car in park. I looked down at my phone. I had a text message from my friend Chris: "Widmann, where'd you go??? You left the shots here I ordered for us. Katie and I are waiting for you."

"Gahh!" I said in mild frustration, turning my head to look around the car. "Do you guys want to go back quick? Chris says he has a shot there for us to take."

"Yeah, sure. Let's do it," they said.

We arrived back at the bar, took the shots, said thanks and goodbye again, and were literally back in my car within five minutes. I pulled back out of the parking lot and saw the light ahead of me was red. Instead of waiting like any other person would, I took a shortcut through the parking lot to my left ahead of the stoplight. The freshly laid, untouched snow covered the lot, and I pulled my e-brake in the wide-open lot to allow my back end to spin around and fishtail before I corrected it and pulled out of the parking lot. I pulled up to the stop sign and slowed down. My car had nearly came to a full stop just as an explosion of blue and red color colors in my rearview mirror caught my attention, along with the muttering of, "Oh shit, dude." from my roommate sitting in the passenger seat of my car. My stomach immediately sank into the floor of my vehicle; my palms were instantly soaked in sweat, my heartbeat shot through the roof, my anxiety was redlined, and my brain, as if acting on its own accord, instantly decided that between fight and flight, flight provided me my best chance at survival.

In my split-second reaction, I thought only one thing: *I can't get caught.* In almost no time at all, my mind somehow ran through every possible consequence: What would I tell my parents? My brothers would think I was an idiot. I might get kicked out of the Army. I couldn't afford these fines. What would everyone think of me? *I've done this hundreds of times—certainly I must be dreaming, surely I must be invincible or above the law. My mental state can't take this right now. Could my life get any worse? I simply cannot get caught. I can outrun him . . .*

I blew through the stop sign, pressing the gas pedal hard enough to accelerate as quickly as possible but not so hard as to spin the tires. Immediately the red and blue lights lit up the otherwise quiet and peaceful city streets behind me. I glanced back to the rearview mirror, noticing the officer had gone through the stop sign and was much closer than I had anticipated he would be.

"Jake, they got you, dude. Just pull over," Rick said.

"Dude, shut up!" I said, gritting my teeth, leaning forward, and gripping the steering wheel like someone was trying to pry it from my hands.

"Jake, dude. You're done. Just pull over," he said again.

"Rick, stop! We'll be fine!" I snapped, leaning forward, focused on the road ahead.

"Holy shit, Jake!" my friend yelled from the back seat.

"Everyone just shut the hell up. I got this," I said, in part to quiet the distracting pleas of reason from my friends but mostly to convince myself that I would be able to create enough separation between myself and the cop that I could make it to the safety of my home.

I pulled my e-brake to ensure that my back end would spin around on the slick streets to successfully make a right turn that I was otherwise going too fast to maneuver. I stomped back on the gas and quickly hit sixty miles per hour in the residential area, now just over a mile from my house. Sporadic glances into my rearview mirror revealed that the distance between myself and the police car behind me hadn't increased, but I was still fast on the gas. I had another three or four blocks to go before I had to make the left turn onto my road. I made note of the streets leading up to mine so as to be prepared to make the turn. I used my brakes as much as my excessive speed would allow and then pulled my e-brake at the last minute to whip my back end around, successfully making the left turn onto my street. Trees and mailboxes lined the road, but somehow I managed to keep my car nearly perfectly in my lane, as if shooting a scene for a new *Fast and the Furious* movie. I was two blocks from my house. I looked ahead, spotted my house, and aimed toward my driveway, cutting across the road at an angle. At thirty miles per hour, I pressed my foot onto the brake, pulled the e-brake, and slid over my driveway into my neighbor's yard. I let the e-brake finish stopping my vehicle as I simultaneously unbuckled, grabbed my keys, and opened my car door to dash for the front door of my house.

I jumped past the three stairs onto our porch and fumbled with my keys, trying to get them into the door handle, awaiting the insertion of my key to unlock it. The keys rattled as my hands shook and I closed one eye to focus on the keyhole to minimize the effects of the alcohol impairment. I grabbed the correct key, shaking as I guided it toward the keyhole. I moved my other hand to the doorknob in order to open the door in unison with its successful unlocking. This whole time I didn't have a fraction of a second to look back and see where the officer was, but I believed I was making good time. I struggled to push the key all the way into the keyhole. Did I have the correct . . . I didn't have time to finish my thought.

"Get on the ground before I tase you!" the cop shouted, close enough that I knew he was within range to do so. The keys dropped from my hands and fell onto the wooden steps as I raised my arms above my head.

"Walk back slowly down the steps!" Unlike the flashing lights I had failed to abide by as I blew through the stop sign, the taser was all the motivation I needed to do exactly as he commanded. I slowly . . . walked . . . backward . . . down . . . the steps. The officer grabbed my wrists before I was off the last step, forcing me to the ground in some sort of well-rehearsed, karate-like move. He handcuffed me and let me lie there with my stomach pressing against the cold, snow-covered pavement.

I raised my head from the concrete and noticed that my neighborhood looked like a holiday parade where the entire police force came out to show support. Only, in this instance, they were showing support for their fellow officer, who had just been led on a two-mile chase through town. The reality of what had just happened hadn't set in yet. The adrenaline rushing through my body, along with the tolerance I had built up by daily heavy drinking, gave me a sense that I was quite sober when I was anything but.

"Sir, can I put my shoes on?" I asked the officer. They had apparently slipped off while I was running up to my house, but I failed to notice until my feet became cold from the frigid Wisconsin air.

"No! Shut up and lie there!"

Eventually he assisted me to my feet to gather my shoes. He and another officer escorted me to a police car, where I would be held while the officers searched my car and questioned my friends. I watched the officers search my vehicle from the warm, plastic bench seat in the back of the police car. My hands were cuffed behind my back tightly and, not surprisingly, uncomfortably. I sat in that police car watching what felt like the best-executed episode of Ashton Kutcher's *Punk'd*, still oblivious to the fact that I wouldn't be sleeping in my own bed that night.

Eventually another officer came to the car. "Can I get you anything?" the young officer asked me before getting in the driver's seat.

"I'm okay right now. Thank you, though," I replied. He began pulling away, retracing the path which I had, no more than an hour prior, led his fellow officer through on a high-speed chase through my hometown. I watched my friends look on in disbelief as I was driven away in the back seat of a police car.

It was a weird feeling—living a scenario I had never imagined, having thought I was invincible for many years, still being intoxicated, and ultimately, not knowing how the remainder of my night would go. I knew very little at this point in my life, but I was certain that this was never a part of my plan. Granted, I didn't necessarily have a plan—but if I did, sitting handcuffed in the back of a police car wouldn't have been a part of it.

MAKE THE CHOICE TO DO MORE, BE MORE, AND NEVER GIVE UP HOPE

While deployed, I spent a fair amount of time thinking about what I wanted to do when I returned home. Nothing was written down or planned out on the pages of a notebook. Rather, I kept it all in the back of my mind as things I would pursue once my "making up for lost time" came to an end. Yet here I was, many months after those plans were already supposed to have been implemented, facing what I would later learn were charges of a DUI and fleeing an officer.

It's interesting to think about what makes someone overcome adversity, create massive success, conquer immense challenges, or live a life that positively impacts the world. Equally as interesting to ponder are the very things that keep someone at these varying levels of success or adversity long term. What are the elements that make someone live a profoundly impactful life instead of a mostly ordinary and fruitless life—or, worse yet, a depressing, regret-filled one?

It would be quite easy to sit down and list off dozens of reasons why people live a life on either end of the spectrum. But that list would only serve to generalize a wide array of people with countless backgrounds, stories, experiences, struggles, and victories. What's better is focusing in on yourself and your story. If you can be honest with yourself about your background, story, experiences, struggles, and victories, you'll have a much better shot at living a life that matters instead of one riddled with disappointment.

Being honest with yourself means looking at your life from a reasonable outsider's perspective, reflecting on it, and then determining the true role you played in creating it. Was it really [insert random person's name]'s fault you got caught, or was it yours? Are your family's history, beliefs, and judgment of you just excuses you grasp tightly so that you don't have to feel the painful regret of not pursuing the life you truly want to live? Is it the casino's fault you gambled away your paycheck, or is it yours? Is it your wife's or attractive coworker's fault you cheated, or is it yours? Is it Starbucks's fault you order a pail of sugar with your espresso, topped with whipped cream and caramel, or yours? Is it Netflix's fault you watch six hours of TV a night and then complain about your life, or is it yours? Some of these forces undoubtedly do questionable things to ensure you overindulge—I'm not denying that, but ultimately it comes down to one person—you. You're going to have to devote some time to this, and it's going to require being brutally honest with yourself and embracing something I call absolute ownership.

Absolute ownership is claiming responsibility for every choice you've ever made and ever will make. Could you have been peer pressured, marketed to, or motivated by external forces? Yes. But ultimately, your decisions are your own. This isn't about pushing guilt onto you for your choices; it's about freedom. Claiming absolute ownership for your choices is the definition of freedom. I've witnessed and felt its impressive benefits firsthand.

The questions above and the many more included in the guide are ones that I've asked myself throughout the years and often find myself referring back to for guidance. Unfortunately, sitting handcuffed in the back of a police car wasn't enough motivation for me to start asking myself these questions. Believe it or not, that event was not rock bottom but only another big stumble on the way to my life's complete collapse. It was the events that unfolded after being hauled away in a cop car that brought me to a place where I had no other option but to reflect on the life I had been living.

"Before I ask you
to sit with me,
I must first be able
to sit with myself.
Before I ask you
to accept my pain,
I have to accept
the pain myself.
Before I ask you
to love me,
I have to be madly in
love with myself."

C. Thoth

4

LEARN ALL YOU CAN FROM YOUR PAST TO BUILD THE LIFE YOU DESERVE

YOU'RE NOT ABOVE THE CONSEQUENCES OF YOUR ACTIONS

I struggled to open my eyes and face the reality that I knew awaited me once I looked up from my "mattress"—a worn-out blue cushion atop a cement bed jutting out from the wall. I was mostly immobile, as my whole body had gone numb from sleeping on a literally rock-hard surface. I knew where I was, but I thought that maybe, if I spent enough time wondering why I made the choices I did, I could have a do-over, like restarting a video game right after you mess up so it doesn't autosave your progress, sparing yourself from dealing with the consequences of a poor decision or mistake. I so badly wanted it to be a mirage, a dream, a horrible joke, but the faint sound of unfamiliar voices—not to mention my cement bed and the shiny metal sink, mirror, and toilet just feet away—clued me in that this was my current reality.

Using my hips to reposition my dead arms, butt, and legs, I successfully rolled from my stomach to my back. I lay there, looking at the high ceilings, waiting for my body to regain feeling and mobility. Sunlight was shining through the small, barred window covered in a frosted film that I assumed was to prevent any communication with the outside world. I thrust my shoulder upward and flung my arms around in a process that must have looked like I was trying to high-five someone with my shoulder only. It allowed me to swing my still half-asleep arm over my body as I sat up onto the edge of my bed. I peered out between the vertical metal bars with my eyes coming into focus on a sign that read, "The Prison Rape Elimination Act of 2003." The print was too small to read any further, but it was enough to allow reality to settle in—my string of "successful" drunken driving had come to an end.

The memories from the four or five hours prior to arriving in jail were still vivid, but part of me still expected someone to intervene in this moment and say, "Just kidding! This was just to teach you a lesson. You don't actually have to stay here. We only wanted to scare you. You're free to go now, but stop being dumb."

I remembered going to the hospital for my blood draw and running into a friend from high school who was on a police ride-along. I assumed she, too, was there because she got into trouble, but she was only interested in catching people like me doing bad things. I didn't have much to say once I realized this. Obviously, it was awkward sitting there in handcuffs trying to make small talk with an old, well-behaved friend. My blood was drawn at the hospital and my mugshot taken at the local police station, and then I was transported and booked into our county jail, where I now sat.

I jumped when I heard a loud click that echoed throughout my cellblock—the doors from the individual cells within it began to open, jolting me out of my hopeful daydream. Two guys made their way to the picnic table that sat in the middle of our cellblock. I observed from my bed, remaining as silent as I could to stay unnoticed. I knew nothing of how to carry myself in jail, and damn sure wasn't trying to do anything that would bring me to anyone's attention.

If there's one thing I knew, it was that I was not the type of person who went to jail. Jail people were icky lowlifes. This stint in jail was only the beginning of me realizing how untrue this belief was. As I would learn, my behavior and actions since I had returned home were on par with, if not worse than, those of the four people I would meet throughout my initial three days in jail.

I eavesdropped on their conversation long enough to work up the courage to step out of my cell and sit down next to my three cellmates. It quickly came to my attention that I was the only one without a prior arrest history. Luckily, the guys I sat next to were more than willing to answer my barrage of questions. There I was, a newly christened inmate at the county jail, sitting next to three others who were relatively seasoned. They told me that my decision to flee from the officer was a felony.

Across the table from me was a guy arrested for skipping bail. Next to me were a guy in for his third arrest for a DUI and a guy arrested for selling narcotics. In light of this new reality, I was able to gain back a bit of my sanity. However, my sanity would soon vanish as the weekend passed by.

Breakfast arrived; we ate and then cleared our area to play spades on the picnic table in the middle of our cellblock. Eventually, the game became boring and my thoughts grew too loud and distracting. I paced the four corners of our cellblock like a lion at the zoo. I had been awake for barely four hours on day one, and I felt like I was losing my mind already. Thoughts of the night before ran through my mind. Ideas of how to move forward flooded my imagination.

My pacing was interrupted by a guard asking me if I would like to make a phone call. *Want to? No. Need to? Yes,* I thought. My family had known it would only be a matter of time before something like this happened. Unlike me, they didn't believe that the lack of consequences for my actions over the years proved I was invincible. Now that I had finally been caught, the reality of picking up a phone and calling someone to let them know I was in jail was anxiety-inducing to say the least. My heart pounded and my palms sweat as I picked up the phone to call my mom. "Jake Widmann," I spoke into the phone, knowing from movies I had watched that this would be relayed to my mom as, "This is a collect call from, 'Jake Widmann,' at the Wood County Jail . . ."

I took a deep breath. "Hi, Mom. . ." I told her I was okay and that I didn't know much else. She asked a few more questions that I didn't know the answers to, and we ended the call. I set the phone back onto the receiver and stood next to it for a few seconds, a little more of my reality settling in.

The following two days dragged on. I played more spades over that weekend than I had in my entire life. After our fourth round of six or seven consecutive games, I needed a break. Pacing wasn't the ideal activity, but it allowed me to ponder what life was going to look like once I was released.

I spent what seemed like an eternity thinking and staring at my feet, having memorized how many steps it took to walk along each wall and complete one lap of the cellblock. I considered that maybe this was the wakeup call I needed to turn my life around and begin living the life I had been talking about with friends while drinking whiskey on the rocks, smoking weed until I couldn't move and nothing mattered.

After lap number fifty-nine, it was back to the picnic table to watch a little TV and play some more spades. We played another five or six games until the combination of boredom and worry for my future took over my mind. Pacing allowed me to control my thoughts better and put them to use, pondering my future and thinking about my choices that night along with all of the other poor decisions that led up to it. After lap number forty-two of that sequence of pacing, I returned to the table to watch the last of the movie, *Cool Runnings*, playing on the small TV mounted from the ceiling.

It was during that pacing that I further explored the lives of my cell-mates, as I asked questions and we all told stories of past choices and mistakes. I slowly realized that this, ending up in jail, could essentially happen to anyone. They weren't inherently evil or bad guys. It began with an initial, inconsequential choice, just as it had for me, and led them to more mostly insignificant choices that became magnified over time and led to an orange jumpsuit inside of the county jail. I went from thinking I was above the law and above others to realizing I was just as capable of getting caught and no better than anyone else.

There were marks on the concrete floor from the hundreds, if not thousands, of other pacing jail members who came before me. They reminded me of when I was a young boy following in my dad's steps where he had compressed the snow ahead of me, making it easier for me to walk. Unfortunately, in this instance, I no longer had my dad's, or anyone else's, footprints to safely guide me from one step to the next. I had been on my own path, and now the steps I was taking were aligned with the thousands of other misguided men who came before me. People who pondered some of the same thoughts, held on to fragments of their hope, and wondered when, or if, they would ever be able to get their lives on track. Just like me, they paced the confines of this cellblock, retracing the steps of the men before them . . . and the men before them . . . and the men before them . . .

I watched the second hand tick endlessly around the clock as I paced from one gray concrete wall to the next and slowly lost more chunks of my sanity. Although it seemed like it never would, Monday finally arrived, and with it came the day I would hopefully be released on bail. It had only been a weekend, but I couldn't handle another day of being trapped where the only daylight I saw was from that small, frosted window I noticed upon waking up my first morning.

In the forty-eight or so hours I had been in the county jail, I'd had plenty of time to think about how I was going to turn my life around when released. Undoubtedly, I was moved by the kind of motivation you can only find on the inside of a jail cell. Not to mention these two days were the longest I had been sober since being home. Thinking with this sense of clarity while cut off from the very things making my life miserable was one thing, but actually committing to the necessary changes while the drugs and alcohol whispered in my ear would be a different challenge altogether. It was easy to say, from the confines of jail, what I would do once I got out, but actually doing those things when faced with the freedom, influences, and routine I had created was going to be more of a challenge than I was dreaming it up to be while pacing from wall to wall.

At eleven o'clock on Monday morning, I returned to my cellblock after talking with the public defender who had been assigned to me. She would be helping me go forward with the charges I was facing, which she informed me, as the guys in my cellblock had, were a DUI and a felony charge of fleeing a police officer.

Soon I would be standing in front of the judge who would determine whether or not I'd be released on bail. Depending on his decision, I would either be walking back to my cell to stay and pace its perimeter an indefinite number of times or be released on bail, free to return home and try to work through this tangled mess of a life I had created for myself.

The guard walked over and inserted her key. The clink of the door unlocking echoed throughout our concrete box. She called us over so we could insert our hands through the waist-high slot to be handcuffed before being transported to our appearance with the judge. One by one, we inserted our hands through the small rectangle opening in the door. The handcuffs clicked as they tightened around our wrists. After the door opened, we exited the cellblock and waited as we each had a chain placed around our waists and attached to our handcuffs so that we couldn't raise our hands higher than our belly buttons.

Minutes later, another door opened and we were led to a bench down the hall. We sat there until we were told to enter the small room ahead of us, where we would stand in front of a screen to communicate with the judge. One of the guys who I was in the cellblock with went before me. After the guard called him in, he stood in front of the screen as the district attorney began reading off his charges. I was able to hear muffled words through the door, "Distribution of a schedule II controlled substance with intent to sell. Possession of cocaine within one hundred yards of a . . ." The district attorney went on with the details of his charges while I wondered if I stood the slightest chance of being let out on bail.

My palms were already dripping with sweat. My knees were weak and wobbly. I attempted to control my breathing to give the appearance that I was put together, but that was anything but the truth. I was as nervous as I'd ever been.

"Jacob Widmann," the guard called.

"Yes, ma'am," I said, standing up, walking my way slowly toward the door she held open for me. I walked in and turned left to stand in front of the old tube television providing me a live, albeit it poor-quality, video feed of the judge and district attorney from within the courtroom.

"Are you Jacob R. Widmann?" the judge asked.

"Yes, Your Honor. I am," I replied, voice shaking. The district attorney stated my charges and the fact that, since I'd fled from the police officer, I obviously had a high potential for jumping bail if I was to be let out. My stomach sank. He had made valid a point that I could hardly argue with. *But please, I can't stay another day here,* I thought, awaiting the judge's response.

"Does Mr. Widmann have any other arrest history?" the judge asked the district attorney to verify.

"No, Your Honor. He does not."

There was a pause. It felt like several minutes. The room I was in was quiet, apart from the shuffling of papers I heard coming through the TV via the courtroom. The judge was looking down at the large wooden podium in front him. "Mr. Widmann," he began, "I'm going to let you out on an absolute sobriety, five-thousand-dollar signature bond. This means you are not allowed to consume any alcohol, to include other substances, or you'll be right back here and be forced to pay five thousand dollars to the court," he said sharply.

I breathed a sigh of relief. "Thank you so much, Your Honor," I said as the guard opened the door for me to be let out of the room and another person let in.

The guard swung the door open and led me back to my cellblock, where I called my brother. Within an hour, I was notified that my brother was there, and I was once again led out of the cellblock area to the reception desk to sign some paperwork and be given back the belongings I had handed in the night I arrived.

"I'm glad you're getting out. You've been the most polite person we've ever had in here," one of the middle-aged guards said to me as she handed me my bag of stuff.

"Hmm," I said, looking ashamedly down at the ground. I replied as appropriately as one can when not sure what to make of a situation. "Thank you. I suppose I try to be."

I'm a polite inmate, I thought as I grabbed the clear bag containing my wallet, phone, and other random items. Those words, in a weird way, forced me to think about the person I used to be and the person I so badly wanted to get back to. The person whom I knew was inside of me and desperately wanted to find once again. I was a polite person. That's how my parents raised me, but never did I expect that to be confirmed by a guard in the country jail.

> *"The secret of change is to focus all of your energy not*
> *on fighting the old, but on building the new."*
> —Dan Millman

IT'D TAKE A LOT MORE THAN JAIL
TO SHAKE AN ADDICTION

The door gave a quick buzz, signaling it was unlocked. I pulled the handle and walked past the waiting area into the more expansive space of the courthouse halls. There stood my brother, Ryan, and his three-year-old son.

"Hey, guys," I said emotionlessly, trying to signify that I knew what I did was wrong but I didn't have any interest in being lectured at the moment. We walked down the hall as my nephew asked his dad for a quarter to get a gumball. He put the quarter in the machine, turned the knob, and put his hand under the opening to catch the gumball as it came rolling out. He popped it into his mouth and, looking up at my brother, said, "Daddy, why are we picking up Uncle Jake from jail?"

My stomach sank. My body warmed from the embarrassment. The room went silent while I awaited my brother's response. What the hell had my life become? I thought as I debated whether I should answer the question for my brother or allow him to handle it. I wanted to cry. Roughly six months ago, I was hugging my family, who had anxiously awaited my return home. Now, my three-year-old nephew, someone whom I'd always wanted to be a role model for, was coming to bail me out of jail. I honestly don't remember who responded to him or what was said, but I know it was simplified into essentially saying that I had made a mistake.

The ride home was quiet. I didn't have much to say. My last three days had been uneventful. A few questions about how I planned to move forward now were asked. I responded with guesses of what I could or should do, but nothing of real certainty. My brother dropped me off, and I thanked him and walked into my house as he drove away.

You would think that an event like this would be the rock bottom I needed to set my path straight. You might also think that an absolute sobriety mandate by the judge would further encourage me not to drink. Unfortunately, addiction is often more complicated and powerful than we realize. It slowly removes the best parts of good people and replaces those parts with black, empty holes, consequently diminishing their hope for a better future. Addiction and routines are much deeper than a simple choice of wanting to make a change. I swear that I badly wanted to make a change, but like many others, I fell into the gap between wanting to change and actually changing. There's much more to overcoming addiction, a long bout of adversity, or any major lifestyle change than just wanting to change.

I no longer had the safety of my jail cell to keep me from drowning my emotions in alcohol and drugs. But I did have friends who were eager to hear about my weekend in jail and a fridge filled with beer.

It's almost unbelievable, isn't it? I was mandated by the court not to drink, and what did I decide to do almost the very second my brother dropped me off at my house? I violated my bail by grabbing a beer and joking with friends while I torched the inside of my pipe, which was empty but covered with the black resin that builds up after you smoke weed out of something countless times. And after you break the terms of your bail once, you slowly forget that there were any consequences in the first place.

◻

This story of me resorting to what I knew best came up a while back, when I was talking with a friend with whom I graduated from high school. It was one of those deep conversations that seem like they could go on forever.

"Shouldn't I have learned my lesson that day when I came home from jail?" I asked him with genuine curiosity, hoping he could provide me some answers based on the experience he also had with addiction.

"I'll tell you this one last story, and then we'll get off of the phone," he said. "I was living away from home with a guy who was helping me stay clean. I had been clean for months and was doing really well helping him around his place and keeping busy. One day, I made a trip home to go to my little brother's soccer game. My parents left the house a little bit before me, and I said I would meet up with them shortly. When I left the house, I had every intention of going to his game, but I felt an intense pull from deep within me, almost like my body made the choice for me without my consent. Remember, I had been clean for a long time. But here I was, stopping by the house that I always knew had good heroin. I went in, shot up, and passed out.

"I woke up in the hospital. I had overdosed. That should have been the literal awakening I needed to get out of that hospital and head back to living with the guy who was helping me stay clean. However, the day I was released from the hospital, I went right back to the house I had just overdosed in, and I got high again."

My body was covered in goosebumps from how much I related to that element of his story. It's one of many stories I've heard that demonstrate the power and inspiration our individual stories have.

"It makes no damn sense. It was the last thing I wanted to do, but I was pulled back so easily," he said, pausing.

"Yeah, it doesn't make any sense. It's almost unbelievable how easily we, and so many others, have fallen back into that routine." We agreed that it was comforting knowing we weren't alone in making those mistakes. Most importantly, it felt great looking back on that period of our life, having now overcome our addictions. Our lives were radically different from the ones we referred to in the stories we had shared on the phone.

◻

Now that I was out of jail, it was clear that I had been proven wrong: I wasn't invincible. I've spent more time than I can recall wondering why I had to be so stubborn—and, really, downright dumb—before I learned my lesson. I took my family's willingness to give me a ride if I ever needed it and traded that offer in for a shake of the dice that only ever guaranteed one thing—eventual defeat.

Shortly after returning home and talking with my family, I decided to let go of my public defender and replace her with a lawyer I believed gave me a better chance of making it past these charges in the best shape possible. I scraped together the last of my money, dipped into the IRA I had set up while on deployment, borrowed fifteen hundred dollars from my brother, and put a lien against my car for twenty-five hundred dollars to retain my new lawyer. I was left with a few thousand dollars to pay living expenses (alcohol included, of course).

Upon meeting with my lawyer, I mentioned to him my tentative plans to move to Ohio, where many of my military friends lived. He advised that it might be good to get away from the life I was living, but that I would need to return for an occasional court appearance.

Ohio was a place I had come to know well over the last two years.

I had been down there several times for training before deploying. During our training and the deployment itself, I became close friends with several people living in the Columbus area. Upon returning home, I had already made several trips to visit those Ohio friends. It was on these visits that thoughts of moving down there began, and once I was finally arrested that thought appeared more necessary than ever.

With that tentative plan in place and a new lawyer handling my case, I loaded up my car for yet another twelve-hour trip to Ohio for a conveniently timed military event—also to look for potential jobs and places to live. I started the weekend by reuniting with the military friends I had recently been deployed with. The mornings and afternoons were consumed by briefings about reintegration into civilian society, searching for jobs, attending college, and other resources to help us be successful. Come to think of it, maybe I should've paid more attention. The one evening we had together, Saturday, was a night filled with drunken shenanigans.

As quickly as Friday had arrived with the excitement and comfort of being surrounded by the people who best understood what I was going through, Sunday would also arrive with feelings of loneliness and doubt that I could actually turn my life around on my own.

> *"People do not realize how important decisions are until they make the wrong ones."*
>
> —Unknown

A CONTINUAL SLIDE TOWARD ROCK BOTTOM

My military family went their separate ways, except for Ben, who was staying a few extra days before flying back to Vegas. The next day, Ben and I decided to go grab some drinks while Allison, whose house we were staying at, went to class. Our plan turned into an all-day drinking disaster.

By the time the night was over, I was—like always—a blacked-out, belligerent mess. I wandered away from the bar my friends and I were at after being cursed out by the bar owner and his girlfriend for leaning on her car. I escaped an epic ass-whooping as well, or so I was told by my friends the following day. Over the next two hours, I haphazardly roamed the streets of Columbus while my friends drove around downtown searching for me.

Not surprisingly, I had gotten angry while talking with my friends as they were looking for me and decided to smash my phone into the pavement. Phone-less and alone, I was left with no viable option to escape the situation I found myself in—wandering the dark, lonely side streets of an unfamiliar city. At about 3:30 a.m., I realized how close I was to spending the entire night wandering. Emboldened by my heavy intoxication and my lack of any resource besides my partially functioning brain, I walked into the middle of the street, stood there, waved my hands over my head, and committed to doing this until a car turned onto this random street in this random neighborhood.

After a few minutes, a car turned onto the road. In what I assume was probably an equal amount of fear and confusion for both them and myself, they stopped a car length away from me.

"Hey guys, I'm not from here. I've been drinking, and my friends, who're driving around the city, can't find me because my phone is broken," I explained. "Is there any way possible you could give me a ride to my friend's house?"

"Ahh, man, I don't know," the driver hesitantly replied.

"Please. I have no other options," I pleaded.

The two guys looked at each other and quietly spoke. "Yeah, I suppose. Go ahead and get in."

I still have no idea why they didn't reverse down the street and leave me there, or drive around me, but something was obviously working in my favor this evening. Maybe it was good karma; maybe they, too, were drunk and thought picking up a lunatic in the street would be a good idea. I tend to believe they were just the nicest guys ever. They allowed me into their car and gave me a ride to Allison's apartment with the help of my shoddy directions.

Once I got back, I went to let myself in, but the door was locked. I proceeded to hit the door with a barrage of knocks, punches, and kicks—all of which went unanswered. *They must be sleeping,* I thought. I started knocking on the window outside the apartment so I could be let in. I failed to notice the intensity of my knocks until my knuckles were bleeding and positioned between the two panes of glass. Failing to assess my actions any longer than a few seconds to notice I was bleeding, I moved over one window to the left, and just as my friends walked to the apartment, I broke that one too.

"What the hell, Jake!?" Allison yelled. I tried to explain, but the frustration aimed my way warranted that I shut my mouth. I bandaged my hand up, and we all went to bed.

The following morning arrived with faint memories that, in my drunken rampage, I had destroyed my phone by slamming it into the pavement, only to pick it up and proceed to bend it in half. I also realized—after scouring my pockets, Allison's apartment (inside and out), and the entire downtown area of Columbus for no less than half a day—that I had lost the only set of keys to my car. I called every municipal office and, after two days, conceded that my keys were officially L-O-S-T. Lost.

Ironically, at this point, I was more lost than my keys were. I was broke. I had more than overstayed my welcome at Allison's place, especially after breaking her windows. I had just kept everyone up until four in the morning looking for me across the vast area of downtown Columbus. I had no option left but to call my brother and ask if he would be able to come get me and my vehicle, twelve hours away, which he did.

Losing my keys, a mistake that for most vehicles would have been an easy fix, wound up costing me around $1,500. Fixing Allison's windows was $450. Getting a new cell phone cost me over $300. Then, add in another $150 to partially reimburse my brother for driving down to

Ohio. A trip that was supposed to be my opportunity to escape from my problems, to start anew, had drained my bank account of any safety net and crushed much of my hope that remained.

Following my mother's wise advice, I'd saved up my money during deployment and returned home with $25,000 in my bank account. All of that money was now in the bank accounts of bars and clubs from Vegas to the Midwest and everywhere in between. It was in the pockets of whoever was willing to sell me weed. It was in the hands of my lawyer, who was fighting to keep me out of jail. The only thing I had left was my vehicle, which I had paid off while overseas but was now only visible on the tow dolly in the side-view mirror as my brother drove us west on Highway 70 out of Ohio.

Almost immediately after returning home, I moved out of my apartment with Rick and into a different one twenty miles away. I was excited for the change; however, my excitement would soon be squashed by the reality that my problems would take much more than a change of scenery to overcome—as if that weren't already obvious from my trip to Ohio.

My bank accounts were constantly being overdrawn. I had only minimal funds coming in from my monthly military duty and the unemployment checks I had applied for about a month prior to being arrested. It left me enough money for food and paying the minimum balance on my credit card and other essential bills.

In short, I knew that I needed a job. Any job. I began working as a vacuum cleaner salesman. It was one of those jobs you find on Craigslist that have zero employment qualifications and for which all you have to do is show up wearing clothes to be trained train you to do whatever it is vacuum cleaner salesmen do. My employment there lasted about a week, and then I realized my inability to sell anything—let alone an overpriced vacuum cleaner—to people who couldn't afford it wouldn't be converting to a livable income.

In the weeks that followed, my mom helped me get a job at a business where she knew the owners. I was hopeful that this opportunity would be the structure I needed in my life—a reset, perhaps. My keen ability to mask the inner damage I carried with me everywhere I went allowed me to interview like I had it all together. I was hired, and began showing up the following week at eight o'clock in the morning for my first real civilian job in years.

I truly thought this would be the break I needed. I would be able to inch closer to a recognizable path, replenish my increasingly negative bank accounts, and regain some trust from my family. However, I quickly realized that this job—any job, really—would only serve as a short-term bandage for the problems I was suffering from internally. From the time I was hired, I sat in my chair for eight hours a day and struggled to focus on anything but the misery my life had become, along with the pending consequences of my arrest.

Within the first week, I was already being talked to about my lack of focus and continual, costly mistakes. I contacted a friend who I knew was prescribed ADHD medication and purchased some from him so that I could focus and perform my job at an acceptable level. My mind was my worst enemy while I sat at my desk, repeating the same task over and over for my entire shift. I soon had to tape a piece of paper over the time on the computer—watching it go by, minute by minute, was turning eight-hour days into never-ending periods of torture.

By my third week, I had already called in twice for bogus reasons so that I could look for a different job. My after-work routine—going home to make dinner and drink alone until I passed out—was getting old. On Thursday of my third week, I'd had enough of the same old same old, both at work and at home, so I drove to a nearby city to hang out with friends.

What began as a night of getting high and going out to the bars turned into me waking up Friday morning at an unknown time in an unknown location. Fortunately, this time it wasn't a jail cell, and I wasn't waking up to a sign that said "Prison Rape Elimination Act of 2003." But the hard surface I'd claimed as my bed left my limbs just as numb as the cold, hard concrete. My phone was dead, and I had no idea where I was, but I knew I certainly shouldn't have slept here.

I sat up, looked to my left, and saw an entire wall of liquor bottles behind the long bar area. *How the hell did I just pass out in the corner booth inside of a bar?* I thought, amazed.

"How . . . ?" was becoming all too common of a question in my life.

I sat at the edge of the booth with the big, tinted picture window to my back. I looked down to notice I was only wearing my boxers and socks. I knew that I needed to get out of there immediately in case someone arrived and thought that I had broken in. I roamed the bar for ten minutes before I eventually found my clothes upstairs, outside of the bathroom.

"Please no one come in here. Please no one come in here. Please no one come in here," I said with clenched teeth, angry but focused as I dressed myself for what I suppose you'd call an escape. *I'm not even supposed to be drinking, let alone what looks like breaking and entering,* I thought. *If I get caught, my life is over.*

After putting my clothes on, I unlocked the front door and walked out. I walked back to my friend's house to charge my phone and get my car. It was 10:45, nearly three hours after I was supposed to be at work. I couldn't believe I had done this. I rang my supervisor and nonchalantly told her I be would arriving in the next forty-five minutes.

"That won't be necessary, Jake. You don't need to come in today," she replied with a noticeably annoyed tone of voice.

"Oh, I don't?" I said, acting surprised.

"Actually, I'm going to have to let you go. Have a good day and best of luck, Jake." Click.

I was overwhelmed with a mix of questions: *What the hell am I going to tell my mom? How am I going to find another job that pays twelve dollars an hour? What am I going to do now?* But I thanked God I didn't have to sit in front of that computer anymore with the darkest thoughts that had ever entered my mind, wondering if that was all there really was to life. I went back and forth between being relieved and worried. It felt great that that job had ended. However, my mom had helped me get that job, and I would eventually have to deal with her disappointment for putting her reputation out there only for me to disrespect those efforts. Again, I was unemployed, still in debt, and responsible for paying rent, bills, and pending fines.

> "Someone I loved once gave me a box full of darkness.
> It took me years to understand that this too, was a gift."
> —Mary Oliver

WHEN HOPE HANGS BY A THREAD

Once again, I found myself wondering, How had my life come to this? I drove home, shut the door to my house, and sat on the cold leather couch with a glass of wine, the only alcohol I had left. I picked up the little pipe I had in hopes that I could get high off of the residue that remained from the hundreds of times it had been packed with marijuana before. I felt sorry for myself and saw no end to the pain that consumed me daily. Over the next few days, I switched back and forth between playing video games, looking for jobs, and drinking whatever alcohol I had left in my house.

A week had gone by, and I had yet to tell my mom I had been fired. I couldn't bring myself to do it. Although I knew she would soon find out, I chose to cross that bridge only when forced.

After roughly a week, I found what I thought to be the answer to my problems: a good job with a great team of people selling life insurance. I was and still am the furthest thing from a smooth salesperson, but I believed in the people I would be working with and thought it might work out.

On the day of my interview, I grabbed my keys and wallet and, before walking out the door, put on the mask I had grown accustomed to wearing anytime I left the privacy of my own isolated, unbearable existence. It was the mask that allowed me to smile, laugh, and tell anybody the stories they wanted to hear. A mask that concealed the person I truly was at that time with the person people needed me to be in any given situation. It was similar to the mask I wore when interviewing for the job I was just fired from. (The topic of masks is an entire book by itself. Luckily, it already exists. I highly encourage you to read *The Mask of Masculinity* by Lewis Howes. It's equally as beneficial for men and women.)

After an in-person interview and a few phone calls, I was hired. The next step was to take a trip two hours south to Madison, Wisconsin, for a class on the basic knowledge needed to acquire the license to sell life insurance.

It was a two-day class, but since it was only two hours from my hometown, I didn't want to pay for a hotel. After class was dismissed, I grabbed some food and drinks at a nearby brewery while texting some friends who lived in the area to see if I could stay at their place. I learned they were all out of town, and I decided I'd sleep in my car. The eating stopped, but the drinking didn't.

At some point in the night, I made nice with a middle-aged couple. We drank until just before midnight and, luckily, those strangers—err . . . friends?—babysat me and took my near-comatose body back to their house to crash on their couch. I was woken up the next morning by the man from the night before. He let me know that I needed to wake up so he could give me a ride to my car and I could get to my class on time.

I finished my class that afternoon and made my way home with forty dollars in cash left to my name. On the rare occasion I checked, I was never surprised to find all my bank accounts were all overdrawn and my credit card was maxed. Aside from the pending final check from the job I'd just been fired from, I was beyond broke. I wasn't only financially broke but emotionally drained as well. I took a good look at my current state and realized the pointlessness of sitting through those two days of classes; I wouldn't be able to pay the two hundred and fifty dollars needed to take the test for my insurance sales license.

The day was almost over, and like all the others before it, I floated as the limp, emotionless, shell of a Jake who once stood proud and happy to simply be alive. Before calling it a night, I grabbed one of the two twenties from the center console of my car and walked from my apartment to the bar across the street. *Dinner and a few drinks,* I told myself, as though I were giving myself a pregame pep talk.

I was finishing my drink and the last few bites of food when the bartender, an acquaintance from high school, said, "I'm getting off soon, and me and a few other people are going next door to drink. You should come with."

I had no plans, so I told him, "Yeah, I will. But I won't be drinking much, if any, because I committed to only spending the twenty dollars I brought with me."

"No worries, man. Just come hang out," he replied.

I woke up the next morning with only a highlight reel of memories, a dry mouth, and a pounding headache. I remembered walking down the sidewalk to the bar next door. I remembered that it was closed, but the owner had apparently allowed us in to hang out and party. I faintly remembered smoking something out of an aluminum foil pipe. That was my last memory: hanging out with some sketchy people, smoking what I believed to be weed out of a handmade pipe, and blacking out.

I looked up at the ceiling wondering how and when this cycle would end. How could everyone I knew go out and control themselves when they drank? I used to be able to do that. I could handle myself better at fourteen then I could now. Now, it felt as if I were drinking simply because I wanted to try and prove myself wrong—I could go out, enjoy myself, and not black out. Unfortunately, it was a challenge that defeated me every time, blackout after blackout.

I knew it was up to me to make the changes necessary, but I had no idea how to break free from this cycle of self-destruction. I scraped together the energy to twist my body out of bed. I showered, brushed my teeth, shaved, and was soon opening the door to my car to go get some gas and a few groceries with my remaining twenty-dollar bill.

I sat down in my car and opened my center console to put my keys and wallet in as I always did. "What the hell?!" I said out loud. *Where did my twenty dollars go? Did someone steal it? There's no way I came back here last night and took it out. Someone had to have taken it,* I thought in disbelief. *Did I really get so drunk last night that I came back to my car and took out the money so I could drink more?* I never failed to surprise myself with the new levels of despair I could plummet my life into. Hope is a precious resource that, in this moment, was hanging by a thread.

ROCK-BOTTOM: ADJECTIVE —
1.) AT THE LOWEST POSSIBLE LEVEL

I opened my car door again, stepped out, and walked back into my house. I unlocked the door and sat down on the cold leather couch in my living room, wondering how this had become my reality. I had been teetering on the edge of rock bottom for the past month or two. I slammed my fists down on the coffee table in front of me. Just like my fists hitting the table, I had crashed hard into rock bottom. I just didn't realize it until later.

Mostly, it was me refusing to believe it, because there were other events before this that should have forced me to straighten my path sooner. I certainly wished that those earlier events were rock bottom; that would have saved me time, money, and loads of stress.

Rock bottom itself is subjective. What may be one person's lowest point could be for someone else just the edge of decline. Ultimately, I think it's the point at which one runs out of resources—physically, emotionally, and psychologically—and realizes that the choices they've been making need to change in order for their life to change. That was exactly true for me. I didn't have a single resource left to cling to in hopes that I could prolong the inevitable for another day.

Looking back, it still seems odd that accidentally spending this last twenty dollars was the last straw. You wouldn't think that twenty dollars would do you much good when you have overdrawn bank accounts, a maxed-out credit card, debt owed to multiple people, and pending fines. Maybe it was the principle that I had committed to not spending that last bill and that I couldn't even keep a promise to myself anymore. Maybe it was a sort of symbolism. Maybe it was the perfect storm and timing that caused me to finally realize I needed to make changes if I was ever going to come back from this. Maybe, of all the chances I had to begin turning my life around, this was the one I would choose.

In that moment, for the first time since coming home from Kuwait, I took time to thoroughly reflect on the choices I had been making. Before this, there had been no thinking or reflecting. There was only doing and then reacting to what my actions brought me.

That brings me back to this book's opening. Sitting on the couch, numb, hearing only the sound of my beating heart—a version of me that I wanted to be hovered above, looking down not in disgust but in hope and belief that my journey wasn't over. Although I had undoubtedly tangled my life into that useless ball of yarn, unlike many other people, I didn't dare think that I couldn't become useful once again.

With no money and little hope for a better future, I sat on that couch pondering ways I could climb out of this hell. It was only me, the subtle whoosh of an occasional car passing by on the street outside my house, and all the memories of the past nine months racing through my head. Once again, I came back to the question—How?

How had I gotten to this exact point? How did my life get this bad? How in the world could I ever let this happen? How was I going to become more if I couldn't go a day without burying my emotions under bottles of alcohol and filling my lungs with weed smoke? How was the question, and I knew now more than ever that alcohol and drugs could no longer be the answer.

I remained on the couch trying to determine a step different from the next one in my normal routine—grabbing the nearest substance and suppressing my thoughts, feelings, and emotions with it. I remembered the bag I had on the windowsill behind me. It was filled with stuff I had bought from Walmart a few weeks back. I knew the receipt was in there.

Aha! I thought. *I could return it. That's an easy thirty or forty dollars.*

In that moment, something clicked. A shift occurred, and the possessions I once used to drown out the noise, distractions, and pain no longer brought me joy. I looked at the PS3 that sat on my TV stand and the wireless speaker I had bought a month ago. I knew I had kept the receipt for the speaker in the junk drawer. I could probably sell my PS3 and games for some money, and I could return the speaker for the hundred dollars I paid for it.

I got everything ready, put it in my car, and drove around town, returning stuff and pawning off the rest. Soon, I had a full tank of gas and some groceries in my refrigerator. I listed on eBay the months-old, two-thousand-dollar TV I bought for myself around Christmas time. The TV was a clear example of thinking that a shiny new object would solve my problems for me, but it only created more. It would be a few weeks before I would have the money I sold the TV for. I used half of it to pay off the remaining balance of the TV—which I purchased on credit—and the rest to bring my bank account balances back into the black.

For the first time in a long time, I was somewhat proud of myself. I had actually done something that made my life better. It felt good taking full ownership of my life. Getting rid of things that I was using to drown out my thoughts was the first of many steps that I had to take in order to remove the ugliest parts of myself and replace them with ones that would help me get to where I wanted to be.

Thoughts, feelings, and emotions are valuable elements of life that must be dealt with. Our problems are going to persist until they're faced head on. Yes, it's imperative that we keep moving (hopefully forward) and resist feeling sorry for ourselves, but suppressing a thought, feeling, or emotion is the last thing I would recommend to someone who wants to make it past a particularly difficult time.

If you're in a period of adversity, stop and take time to reflect on the choices you've made that have gotten you to the place you're in. If you take the time to do that, I'm certain you'll gain the clarity you need to shift your mindset and take back control of your life.

REFLECTION IS THE KEY TO DOORS THAT
OTHERWISE WOULDN'T HAVE BEEN OPEN

I used to lie in bed at night, staring at the ceiling, anxiously wondering how I was going to make it past this period of my life and on to a better future. I knew that it was possible, and I always remained hopeful I'd one day get there, but I knew nothing about the amount of work it would take or what those first steps to a better life would look like. Teachers and parents tell us to think before we act or speak, but I always thought that was their way of getting me to talk less. Now, I wish I would've implemented it when I was younger in hopes that I could've avoided some of the mess I found myself in now. I was simply going from day to day, reacting in surprise to the inevitable consequences of my actions.

Reflection gave me the answers to the questions I desperately wanted to understand: Shouldn't coming home from jail have been rock bottom? Why didn't I resolve to turn things around when I held a piece of paper that commanded "absolute sobriety"? How come I couldn't drink like most normal adults? It was when I understood the honest answers to these questions and many more that I was able to change.

For me, rock bottom was an abstract place that only showed itself when I had fully run myself dry of all resources: money, ideas, employment, relationships, and belief in myself. The only resource that remained was the will to make better choices and the hope that one day my life would be better than it currently was.

The realizations that reflection led me to were what motivated me to make it a daily practice in my life. I realized that it wasn't only the absence of money that forced me to change. It wasn't only waking up the mornings after embarrassing myself beyond belief. It wasn't only the three painfully slow days in jail. It wasn't only my family and friends' desire for me to figure things out. It was all of it. Every single one of those things, and many others, led me to begin turning my life around.

As Ryan Holiday says in *Ego Is the Enemy*, "I'm not someone who believes in epiphanies. There is no one moment that changes a person. There are many."

I heard that while listening to his audiobook and couldn't help but pause his narration and ponder those words a bit longer. It's so true. It wasn't one moment, idea, realization, mistake, or any other single thing that forced me to begin turning my life around. Often, one moment can bring everything into perspective, and while it's easy to give credit to the one moment that catalyzed everything, it's hardly ever one moment alone that forces change.

I can't possibly sit down with everyone going through tough times, much like my best friend did with me when he asked, "Jake, what the f*ck are you doing with your life?" What I can do is put my story out there for others to read, and tell you that when you get to that point where you're sitting on a cold leather couch with your head resting in your palms, ready to slam your fists down on the table, you need to take some time to really think—about the choices you've been making, the life you've been living, and, ultimately, the life you know you want and deserve.

In that moment you'll realize that, no matter how bad your situation might be, you're exactly where you are because of the choices you've made for yourself. It's not the officer's fault I was arrested for driving drunk. It's not the fault of the people who submitted the urinalysis I failed before deploying. It wasn't my roommate's fault that I drank and smoked weed everyday. It wasn't my family's fault that I destroyed their faith in my ability to be a responsible adult. It's not the world's fault that life is hard.

Everything. Everything you've ever done, both right and wrong, is your fault. I'm not saying this so that you can feel incredibly guilty and paralyzed. I'm saying this because you are the only element in your life that you have control of, and taking ownership of all that you have done and will do is surprisingly empowering. It might not seem that way now, because your past is something you'd rather dissociate from rather than own up to, but I promise you it's essential. In one year, two years, five years, when your life is unrecognizable from what it is now, you'll realize how crucial and liberating the decision to take ownership of your entire life was, rather than remaining a victim of it.

It's interesting to reflect on our lives and think that if only we would have acted differently in a period of time, then some major event, possibly the one that led you to pick this book up, wouldn't have happened. Life, no matter where you are currently, is made up of an incalculable number of decisions from the time we are aware of our existence until now and every second going forward. It's made up of the decisions we did make, the decisions we didn't make, and the decisions we let someone else make for us. Every single one of those instances has led us to the exact place we find ourselves currently. Wherever we might currently find ourselves, it's interesting to think about the alternative choices that were there to take. That is to say that you always have the option between constructive and destructive choices and those everywhere in-between, and I hope you'll do your best to choose those that move you closer to the person you want to become. I hope you'll think about that for a second and keep it as a focal point of your life going forward. Nonetheless, there's an entire chapter devoted to this later in the book.

I stood up from the couch that day and put one foot in front of the other, and for the first time in years I took my finger, which I had pointed in every direction possible, and returned it to the only place it ever belonged: pointing back at me, staring me down like the barrel of a revolver in a game of Russian roulette, where my only choices were to pull the trigger and hope for the best or to stand up and yell, "I've had enough!" That finger forced me to be honest with myself if I was ever going to overcome consequences of the choices I had been making.

I had finally reached the point where I couldn't stand waking up to the life that I was choosing any longer. My life had become filled with so much misery that changing no longer seemed like an elusive obstacle but was instead a mandatory checkpoint to get to the self I aspired to be.

> *"Change happens when the pain of staying the same is greater than the pain of changing."*
> —Tony Robbins

It's not enough to want a better life; you have to do something to improve it. When I returned from my deployment, I had plans. But instead of executing them, I quickly picked up a beer and began searching for happiness and meaning at the bottom of it. And when I didn't find it there, I moved on to the next one.

Yet here I was . . . about a week into making noticeable moves toward a better life and being rewarded with a better attitude, less stress, and revitalized hope. I was on the path to making better choices, but I couldn't help but step off it to go visit a friend in a nearby city who I knew was "celebrating" April 20—an unofficial holiday for weed smokers. We sat around the coffee table, getting unimaginably high. I was a notorious lightweight and fell out of the rotation long before everyone else was done smoking. I melted into the couch and zoned out to the music filling the room. I was in my own little world, practically unconscious but alert enough to be quickly jolted back to the present moment when my phone began vibrating in my pocket.

It's my mom, I thought as I frantically worked to pull my phone from my pocket. *She's going to be pissed if I don't answer and assume that I'm doing something I shouldn't be. But if I do answer, she's going to know that I'm doing something I shouldn't be . . .* Running through possible scenarios of getting caught had become an annoying tradition.

I stood up and ran to the back bedroom, where it would be quieter. I looked at my phone to see who was calling me and exhaled a breath of relief. It wasn't my mom. It was a high-ranking soldier from my Army unit. I usually wouldn't have answered this call while high, but something brought me to push the round green button on the screen and, as casually as possible, say, "Hello, this is Jake."

"Specialist Widmann, this is Sergeant First Class Hairston," he began.

"Hey, SFC Hairston. How're you?" I said cheerfully, attempting to mask my dry mouth and slightly irregular speech—the effects of being high.

"I'm doing well. Listen, we had someone drop out of the deployment to Afghanistan and now have a spot open for you if you want it," he said matter-of-factly.

"Oh my gosh! Really? Yes, I definitely do. Well . . . let me talk with my family, and I'll get back to you, but count me in!" I said without giving much thought to what I had just tentatively committed to.

"Okay, sounds good. Talk soon."

I slid my phone back into my pocket and stood alone in that room. I was in a trance. It was literally like in the movies when the person in the scene is tuned out from their surroundings, oblivious to the world around them and perfectly locked in on what has their attention. I could feel the blood pulsing through my body. The beating of my heart drowned out all background noise. A warm sensation overwhelmed me. I felt comforted. From the tips of my toes to the hair standing erect atop my head, I was overwhelmed by a tingling feeling throughout my entire body. The goosebumps covering my skin made it feel like I had a protective barrier surrounding me. I felt at ease. I felt relief. I felt something positive for the first time in a long time.

I was completely locked in on feeling the exhausting emotions that I had been carrying with me for months—anxiety, fear, anger, sadness, pain, disappointment—all being flushed from my body. As they left, I felt the overwhelming warmth grew stronger. I felt a rare sense of comfort, one I'd imagine is only available when you've reached a point as low as mine. I finally knew that it would all be okay, and for that reason alone, my troubles didn't matter as much anymore.

You know when you're having a rough day but can't quite put your figure what's wrong, and then someone close to you comes along, wraps their arms around you, pulls you in, and gives you what feels like the perfect hug? In that moment, nothing matters. You feel safe, protected, cared for, loved, important, and worry-free. As long as their arms are around you, you no longer feel lonely. Instead, you feel like you're an integral part of the world. You are the world and the world is you. You are everything and nothing all at once. That's what that moment felt like, but maybe even more intense due to the dire circumstances of my life at the time.

I stood motionless in that room. I could literally feel the weight from the consequences of my past choices draining from my entire body—through my fingertips, the end of my toes, and every pore—and dissipating into the room I was standing in. Like the smoke that leaves a summer campfire, my anxiety, fear, and despair drifted away from my body until they vanished into the air. I would imagine you might be thinking that the feelings of ecstasy I had experienced weren't genuine, but were instead overshadowed by the fact that I was high. I get that, but I had been high hundreds if not thousands of times before this, and I had never once experienced even a quarter of the euphoria I felt in that moment as every negative emotion I was holding onto for months dissipated into the room around me.

I came back to the sense of reality that was facing me—my response a few minutes ago meant I had just volunteered to go to Afghanistan in the coming months. An opportunity that I had shown interest in a few months ago while conducting my weekend military duty was now likely to become a reality. I'd volunteered for Kuwait because when compared to Iraq or Afghanistan, it was a safe deployment. This time around, I barely thought about the danger. I was determined to make it past the hardship I had put myself in, and if that meant deploying to a country infested with people who wanted me and the rest of my fellow soldiers dead, then so be it. As many times as I had driven drunk and consumed deadly amounts of alcohol, it was only by luck that I wasn't dead yet, and there was no guarantee that I would be able to turn my life around from where I currently stood--high, in my friend's bedroom.

I opened the door, walked back out of the room, and sat down in my spot on the couch. After an hour, I let my friends know that I needed to head home. I called my family on the drive home to let them know about, what to me, was good news. They reluctantly supported my decision. I made one last call to SFC Hairston, letting him know that I would for sure be going on the deployment. I briefly mentioned that I was facing some legal challenges around my likely DUI conviction, and he informed me that we would work through it. I breathed a sigh of relief just as I felt the world breathing a greater sense of hope and life into me. Maybe all I needed to do was want to change my life badly enough that it propelled me to take that first step in the right direction. Whatever it was, I felt it, and finally having traction in the right direction was all the clarity I needed to keep putting one foot in front of the other.

MOMENTUM IS A POWERFUL FORCE

Choosing to take time and plan out your life is crucial if you want to stand a chance at putting your adversity behind you and learning what awaits. A holistic view of your life will show you how the choices you've been making have gotten you to where you are and what choices you need to make to get to where you want to be. That alone will move the needle toward a life that matters as much as anything you devote your time to.

I could see that, now that I had crashed into rock bottom, I was finally standing on solid ground, albeit much below the surface. I concluded that if I was willing to do the dirty work to climb out, then one day the strands of hope I'd held onto all of this time would be the reins with which I would steer myself out. It was because of my reflecting upon everything prior to rock bottom that I was able to begin my journey past it. And it was my reflection while on that journey that always kept me moving forward.

Reflection was the splash of cold water, the slap in the face, the reality check that took me out of my fantasy world where I believed my choices didn't have any consequences and dropped me back into reality to deal with the wreckage I had left behind me. Like switching from reverse to drive, that first step is often the most difficult, energy-intensive part. I didn't have to do much to get myself into a position where I could say yes to that deployment, but I needed to do something. And that's all you need to do right now as well—something.

I've seen quotes on motivational Instagram posts that say things like, "When the past calls, don't answer. It has nothing new to say," or, "Don't look back. You're not going that way." I can't think of any advice that is more useless and downright terrible. Sure, don't focus on the past so much that you're paralyzed from moving forward. Certainly don't ruminate over it so much that you spend all your time regretting the choices you've made. But to not look back is like trying to build a skyscraper with no blueprints and no relevant experience. The past is how you determine what you want and don't want from your life. The past is where you look to decide who you want to be and don't want to be. Without reflection on your past, you're destined to repeat the same mistakes over and over again. I sure did.

You're probably telling yourself right now how hard it is to create the life you deserve while you're filled with doubts. I get it. I also had those thoughts, feelings, and doubts. Trust me: it's possible and unimaginably worth it to put in the work that will move you forward.

What began as the realization that I was the one who was in control transitioned into taking my first step toward the flicker of light that was visible from rock bottom. The momentum that previously dragged me down to the depths was now pulling me back out. After I moved far enough past that hellish period of my life and spent enough time reflecting on it, I actually became grateful for those experiences and the lessons I learned.

When I forced myself to reflect on my past, it brought forth not only a sense of ownership but also the gratitude that I just mentioned. Gratitude has the power to erase your anger, regret, fear, and anxiety. It was reflection that brought me through the adversity, but it was gratitude that allowed me to heal from it and continue creating the life I deserve.

"Let today
be the day
you give up
who you've been
for who you
can become."

———

Hal Elrod

5

GRATITUDE WILL TAKE YOU FURTHER THAN YOU'D EVER IMAGINE

YOU DON'T WANT YOUR LIFE IN SOMEONE ELSE'S HANDS

If I just wanted to tell a captivating story, I would say that dragging myself from rock bottom was a two-year journey filled with bloodied knuckles, blistered feet, and overwhelming pain, sweat, and tears. But, honestly, it was nowhere near that intense.

I made two decisions: I was no longer going to live my life the way that I had been, and I was going to make myself the only thing that mattered to me—not my family or friends, not my career, nothing. I was not only the number-one priority in my life but also the *only* priority. And with those two things, I gained enough clarity to know that if I got my ass off that couch and took even the slightest step in the right direction, I would slowly begin climbing up and back out of the pit of hell I had dug myself into.

That light visible from that pit was now closer than ever. My efforts were noticeable, albeit manageable, and had allowed me to stand up to begin climbing out of rock bottom so that I was able to grasp both hands firmly onto the edge of stable ground. All I needed to do was dig my feet into the side and use my arms to climb out the rest of the way. The only thing preventing me from doing so was a man in a black robe. He could either be Scar from *The Lion King*, grabbing my hands, shoving them from the ledge, and sending me tumbling back down, or he could be the opponent on the football field who reaches out a hand to someone in need and helps them to their feet. In this moment, having my future in someone else's hands was unsettling.

The thought never crossed my mind that one day I'd have to stand in front of a judge and await his decision on my sentencing. Yet here I was, getting ready one early, mid-May morning to appear in court for the sentencing of my offense—fleeing an officer.

From the time I'd hired him until the closing out of my case, my lawyer handled all of the routine court proceedings aside from one mandatory appearance. According to the documentation I had received in the mail from my lawyer a few weeks earlier, the district attorney was pushing for thirty days in jail and a $1,500 fine. This is what he would recommend at sentencing, but it was ultimately up to the judge to determine my jail time and fines. A sentence of thirty days meant that I wouldn't be able to go on the deployment, because they were leaving roughly two weeks from that day to begin pre-mobilization training at Fort Dix, New Jersey. To say that I needed a lot of help was a mega-understatement. Nonetheless, I was ready to put this behind me and reluctantly accept whatever punishment I received. My anxiety was abnormally high from the time I received that packet until I appeared in court, standing in front of the judge to await my sentencing.

On that morning, I woke up early, got ready, and arrived at the courthouse half an hour before my specified time. Before standing in front of the judge, my lawyer called me into a small room outside the courtroom to answer any questions I had and to set some expectations about the judge's possible ruling. We exited the small room through the heavy wood door and quietly entered the empty courtroom to sit down in our designated area in the front.

My sweat-soaked dress shirt felt cold as it pressed between my arms and my side. My face felt warm. I was reminded of my childhood asthma attacks, struggling to catch my breath. I inhaled as deeply as possible, held it, and exhaled as the door to the left of the judge's stand opened up.

"All rise for the Honorable Judge Rudie," the court clerk said. I stood, hearing only the thumping of my heart as it echoed into my ears. I had never been so nervous in my life. I inconspicuously took long, drawn-out, deep breaths to mask my nervousness.

The judge began by asking my lawyer a few questions relevant to me and my case. My lawyer made sure to mention to the judge that I was a veteran who had recently returned from a deployment and that I had no other previous arrests. Then, the district attorney spoke, saying that fleeing an officer is no small offense and needed to be dealt with accordingly. He turned to the judge and stated his recommendation.

The room was quiet, other than the shuffling of some papers and my heart thumping out of my chest. My breathing went from being autonomous to something I had to talk myself through in order to prevent passing out. *Deep breath,* I thought. *Inhale. Exhale . . . quietly.* The several-second pause between the DA finishing and the judge responding felt outrageously long.

"Mr. Widmann," the judge said, pausing.

"Yes, Your Honor," I replied while my knees quivered from beneath the waist-high table.

"I think you're a good man who made some really, really stupid decisions."

I lifted the corner of my mouth as if I was about to say something, but instead nodded in agreement.

"With that being said, I've noticed that the arresting officer has given you a break and the district attorney has given you a break. I'm going to give you a break as well," he said, pausing to look down at the papers in his hands once more.

He continued speaking before I had a chance to process the meaning of what he had just said. "I'm going to reduce your felony charge to a misdemeanor and sentence you to fifteen days in jail, reduced to twelve for time already served, with eligibility for home monitoring. That'll also come with a fine of $650, plus court costs."

My lawyer said, "Thank you, Your Honor," and then looked at me and whispered, "That's really good news." My thoughts were in ten million different places. The words hit me like a foreign language, with no meaning or emotion. I had just received a substantial break, and the only thing on my mind was the fact that I still had twelve days of jail time in my future . . .

"Thank you so much, Your Honor," I said.

Looking back, I'm incredibly lucky to have been given the sentence I received, but in that moment any jail time felt like too much. The three days I had already served were borderline unbearable. Four times that would be excruciating. Fortunately, this roundhouse kick of reality, standing before a real judge, in a real courtroom, with a real(ly expensive) lawyer, showed me that real life isn't about walking through with no consequences. I've realized since that day just how grateful I need to be for that judge and his willingness to give me a lesser sentence.

The judge nodded and dismissed us from the courtroom. My lawyer pointed toward the center aisle and nudged me toward it. We walked side by side out of the courtroom and back into the small room we had left not more than fifteen minutes earlier.

"Going forward, you'll call the county jail to set up a time when you can come in to get your ankle bracelets put on to serve your time," my lawyer said.

"Ankle bracelets?" I asked.

"Yeah. You'll be serving your time at home with home monitoring," my lawyer said.

"What?! No way. That sounds great," I replied. "Thanks for everything! I really appreciate it." My lawyer and I shook hands before going our separate ways.

I walked back out of that small room one last time and made my way outside to my car. I still remember sitting in my car after walking out of the city municipal building that day, thinking about the past several months and how crazy they had been. A year ago I would never have guessed that I would be standing in front of a judge facing a felony charge. Now, I was calling the number printed on my paperwork to immediately pay my fines. I could hardly afford them, but I wanted them behind me.

This moment seemed like the conclusion of one chapter and the beginning of another. For the first time since a month after returning home, I was truly looking forward to the future rather than limping through each day wondering how I was simply going make it to tomorrow.

Now, writing those last few sentences, I realize they go hand in hand with a popular saying: "If you keep doing what you've always done, you'll keep getting what you've always got." I changed nothing, so nothing changed. Then, one day, when I was depleted of the resources I had to continue carrying on the way I had been, I was forced to change. Guess what happened? My life began turning around, and in much less time than we often assume it takes, I began feeling the impact of those better choices and actions I was making.

That's a powerful realization for you as you go through this book. Making different choices usually doesn't take much extra time, money, or energy. It's empowering to gain back a bit of control over your life, little by little, and begin reaping the benefits of those better decisions.

Since the morning that I woke up in jail, I only wanted one thing: for this event and its consequences to be fully behind me. With my fines paid off, I was another step closer to that becoming a reality.

ROCK BOTTOM IS THE FOUNDATION
OF YOUR FUTURE

Realizing that I had mistakenly spent the twenty dollars I promised myself not to spend was an event that forged my decision and commitment to the process of turning my life around. The few strands of hope that remained prior to that event were now much thicker, and new ones had begun forming as well. After high school and throughout my travels in the military, I had learned that life had much more to offer than what I had always thought. The "more" that I wanted to pursue was not yet within reach, but it was now clearly visible.

It was just after nine in the morning, and the sun was beginning to warm the cool, late spring air. I sat in my car, feeling noticeably less anxious. Soon I would be leaving to train for my second deployment, and for the first time in almost a year I was confident that I was doing the things I needed to create the future I had always remained hopeful for.

As I mentioned at the beginning of this book, I began writing with the goal of helping people to avoid adversity, but while writing my first draft I realized how valuable these experiences were to me. I shifted my perspective to view them as lessons rather than burdens or perpetual problems in my life. Right now, you're exactly where you need to be (not to be confused with where you want to be). Whether you believe that last sentence or not, you can't change the past. Wishing it were different only throws away the time you could've utilized to create a better future.

I've found the best way to navigate adversity and use it as a tool instead of a crutch is to be genuinely grateful for the things you've gone through. Yes, the exact things that caused you pain and hardship, cost you money, damaged relationships, and kicked you through the mud—I want you to be grateful for all that. Gratitude is what will allow you to say, "At least I'm no longer . . ." or "At least I still have . . ." or "At least I didn't . . ."

I want to briefly mention this because I think it needs to be said. Last chapter I went in-depth about the importance of reflecting on your life—where you are now, how you got there, where you want to be, and what you need to do to get there. Reflection is something practical and concrete that anyone can do quite easily—you journal, chat with a friend, or go for a walk and ponder your past. But as I wrote this chapter and kept going through the edits, something still felt like it was missing. I realized gratitude is not concrete. It's abstract, and you don't always feel or see its full spectrum of benefits immediately.

I don't want you to get to this chapter and put the book down because you think it's about to be some foo-foo stuff where I incorporate energy healing and tell you to go into the woods to "find yourself." I won't be doing that, but I also won't be telling you that you need to "get over it," or "just deal with." Are there benefits to being out in nature and breathing in fresh air? Absolutely. Are there benefits to having grit and moxie and being able to persevere when things get hard? Absolutely. Are there benefits to being strong when life gets you down? Absolutely. But "getting over it," or "just dealing with it." aren't going to resolve any issues, and that's what we're trying to do here. It's gratitude that is going to help you grow as a person and relieve yourself of the anger, resentment, and fear you may be experiencing.

You have the foundation—a past filled with challenges, adversity, highs and lows, and your own version of rock bottom or a journey close to it—now start building the structure on top of it.

YOU CAN TRY DOING IT ON YOUR OWN, OR YOU CAN USE THE RESOURCES AVAILABLE

Over the next few weeks, I moved out of the house I had rented for only two months and, with a half-hearted approval from my mom, moved in with her and my stepdad for the next few weeks so I could carry out my twelve days of house arrest. I arranged to have my ankle bracelets attached at the end of May, and they would be coming off the day before I had to meet up with my unit to begin training for my second deployment. The timing couldn't have been any luckier.

I went for a long drive to enjoy the air—which hadn't felt so light, fresh, and free in a long time—and found myself wondering what I would do during my time locked down at my mom's house. I had begun a side job doing landscaping that I would be able to go to during the day while on house arrest, but my evenings could no longer consist of consuming alcohol until I passed out. I stopped at the local bookstore to buy a few books to read while I was on house arrest and then made my way to the county jail to have the ankle bracelets attached.

Later that same afternoon, I walked out of the county jail with my new fashion accessories attached tightly to each ankle. I had failed to think about my wardrobe before leaving home, and my athletic shorts showed off my new anklets rather effectively.

Over those twelve days, I would be able to do more reflecting on the past nine months of misery I had put myself and many others through. While reflection was crucial to putting my life in perspective, the largest long-term impact on my life during those twelve days came from the two books I semi-randomly plucked from the bookstore shelves. In all my years prior, the only books I had actually read were the Encyclopedia Brown mystery books in elementary school. I skated through middle and high school without reading any of the required novels by either utilizing the internet to summarize or by discussing them with friends. Yet, in twelve days, I read two books from cover to cover, and to this day I still reference them and refer them to others often.

I think the biggest thing they did was give me permission. They gave me permission to choose and then create the life I wanted to live. They made me realize that I didn't need approval from anyone to do so.

The first book I read was *Start Something That Matters* by Blake Mycoskie, the founder of TOMS Shoes. It showed me the dreams I had of starting a business—or, quite fittingly, something that mattered— really could be done in a way that gave back and made the world a better place. It catalyzed my mind into thinking of ways I could follow through on the principles of his book. It showed me that you could become financially stable, have significance, and make an impact on countless lives, all while creating something that people want. It further fueled the entrepreneurial drive that I'd had when I was younger but had lost as I meagerly gave in to the pressures of society by being "realistic."

The second book was *Steal Like an Artist* by Austin Kleon. It's a rather short book, but the ideas in it are phenomenal. As perfectly summarized on the book's Wikipedia page, Kleon "does not mean 'steal' as in plagiarize, skim, or rip off—but study, credit, remix, mash up, and transform. Creative work builds on what came before, and thus nothing is completely original." This book, if anything, gives people permission to be inspired by others' work and to create by way of adaptation from everything and anything we so choose to be inspired by. Although formal education teaches us that simply pulling an idea from another person's work is punishable with an F, and by further embarrassment for having cheated, this book does away with that archaic belief system.

Those two books by themselves are phenomenal, but when read together they helped give me an extra sense of empowerment and a "can-do" attitude. Combined with my twelve days of house arrest, they further cemented in me the belief I had held all along that there was much more to my (and everyone's) life than just an average, ordinary existence. I realized that I was currently on the right path, albeit with ankle bracelets affixed. Although I still had debt, years' worth of emotional damage to repair, and lots of maturing and reflecting to do, the journey I was on and would continue along was becoming extraordinarily rewarding.

> *"Gratitude makes sense of our past, brings peace for today, and creates a vision for tomorrow."*
> —Melody Beattie

GRATITUDE IS ESSENTIAL TO LIVING A LIFE THAT MATTERS

"Gratitude" was not one of the more frequently used words in my vocabulary back when I was serving my sentence on house arrest. I knew the word and had been told that I "need to be grateful for what I have," but I didn't take the time to truly practice the skill of cultivating gratitude.

I can't remember the first time I felt true gratitude, but it's likely that it came sometime on my second deployment, amongst the hours I had to lie awake in my bed as helicopters flew overhead and planes took off on the nearby runway. Once you experience the true freedom that stems from owning your actions, gratitude is inevitable. If there's one thing that all of this had shown me, it was that I wasn't invincible. I had been warned not to drive drunk dozens of times by people who knew what would eventually happen; either I would get caught or someone would wind up hurt or dead.

Driving drunk had become a routine for me. I accumulated hundreds of experiences behind the wheel at varying levels of intoxication. Sometimes I was so drunk that I explicitly remember asking the next morning, "Guys, how did we get back here?" only to be surprised when finding out that it was me who had driven after reaching a point of intoxication at which my brain decided that forming new memories was less important than breathing, pumping blood, and digesting alcohol.

From the time I had that first drink while camping with my family, I began taking gradual and hardly noticeable steps toward the event that would ultimately lead to the plastic bracelets around my ankles. Each day the hard boxes attached by the ankle strap would knock against my ankles, and while I did notice it, I didn't notice the effects until after they were removed, revealing bruises around my ankles from the tiny, hardly noticeable knocks against them with every step I took. It was the same with my drinking. Each time I drank I did something dumb and noticed it, but I didn't realize the inevitable consequences of the path I was going down until after it was too late and I found myself locked up in a jail cell.

Much easier to notice was that, with each step I took, the bracelets knocked against my ankle, reminding me that, eventually, everyone gets caught. For some, it will be the first time they choose to step over the line. For others, like me, it may be the four hundredth time. Either way, each instance—no matter if it's drinking and driving, doing drugs, gambling, or cheating—comes with its own countdown for each person. When that last grain of sand falls through the hourglass, you'd better be ready to return to reality and begin turning your life around, or you'll fall to the ground as your world continues to crumble around you.

Gratitude is what helped me realize just how necessary and valuable every single one of the experiences I went through was. Hope in a better future for myself kept me moving while I was going through my most difficult times. When I was able to become grateful that I was arrested, grateful that the judge gave me only fifteen days instead of thirty, grateful that I had at least one friend who could look me in the eyes and ask me what the f*ck I was doing, grateful for the choices I made and the lessons I learned from them, a true transformation began. Gratitude requires an open mind and ownership of our actions. Regret requires a closed mind and pity.

Reflection is how I claimed responsibility for my choices—and, ultimately, my life—but anger at the fact that I had ever been caught in the first place still consumed me. Reflection forced that finger to point back at me, and with that came anger for allowing myself to fall so far out of alignment from who I thought I was and wanted to be. I once heard someone say that you can't be angry and grateful at the same time, and that couldn't be truer. When I chose to be grateful, my anger washed away like sand castles at high tide. Better yet, it was replaced by a newfound optimism for my future and the life I knew I was welcome to enjoy if I would work for it.

My gradual climb out of rock bottom began with the tiniest step possible out of desperation and into possibility. Just like the flapping of a butterfly's wings can cause a tsunami halfway around the world, it was that small step that led to an immeasurable number of additional, tiny steps and an overall impact that made my life radically different. Some steps propelled me forward and some sent me back, but I always made progress over time.

TO OVERCOME IS TO COMMIT TO THE PROCESS

Over time: those two words are what you need to focus on. My progress was almost never noticeable when measured by the day, week, or even month. However, it was impossible to ignore that things were changing—that I was changing. You have to trust that if you're doing the right things most of the time, even with occasional slip-ups, you're going to get to where you want to be. For me, nearly five years after I was arrested, I found myself in such a different place that I was able to sit down and write a letter to my arresting officer, thanking him for being the one who finally caught me and apologizing for putting his life in danger the night of my arrest; a conclusion I was able to reach only after having grown and matured to a place where I could no longer deny that my actions did have consequences.

Writing a letter like that is the definition of gratitude, and that's exactly the message that I relayed to him. That letter was me accepting ownership for my mistakes and laying down all of my excuses. I had created so much distance between the person I was during a certain period of my life and the person I had grown into that I could look back and say, "It may not have been pretty, but I sure am glad I went through that and it turned out the way it did—the lessons I learned and the strength I gained will be with me for the rest of my life." When you do that, the anger disappears and your internal wounds heal almost instantly.

Gratitude is what allowed me to forgive myself for letting my life fall apart, and also thank myself for the lessons learned from that journey. It's easy for most people to just say, "I'm grateful for a roof over my head, clean water, and a loving family," but when you look back on your life, stare directly into some of your most painful moments, and are grateful for them, you've reached a special spot that not many will put in the work to get to.

Gratitude, much like the entire process of turning my life around, wasn't something that came overnight. It took me years of work to fully appreciate, respect, and understand the great impact that my choices had on my life. You reading this book and making it this far is proof that you know there has to be more for your life and that you are determined to work for it.

I believe that most people can and will get themselves through the most trying times in life and back to level ground. But, while it's substantially better than a life of pain and suffering, level ground is simply existing. This book is about choosing a life that matters, not choosing a life that just happens.

Finding and then continually practicing gratitude is what will catapult you onto the foundation for the life you want to build. On top of that foundation is where you will build your structure, your unique *more* that you want for your life: more time, more freedom, more love, more honesty, more money, more meaning in your work, more ambition, more impact. Whatever your more is, healing and learning from your past are crucial steps to achieving it. Gratitude will lay the foundation so you can begin building the walls and laying floor after floor on top of it.

NOT ALL MOMENTUM IS EQUAL

Momentum works both ways. Just as we dig ourselves into a hole with mostly routine choices, we dig ourselves out with mostly insignificant victories. Any one isolated thing, good or bad, isn't going to send us plummeting into rock bottom or shooting across the finish line—but when linked together and compounded over time, all these steps have the power to take you almost anywhere. Those painfully slow and boring steps, forward or backward, create momentum, and when enough of it is present, we feel either unstoppable or hopeless.

When I was able to notice things looking up and my overall mental and physical health began improving, it became easier to make the right choices every day. But even so, I still made some of the wrong choices over and over again during the process of putting this period of my life behind me. It's so important that you realize this. You're going to mess up. You're going to fail. If you don't go in with those expectations, you'll give up before you ever have a chance to succeed. You'll be so much stronger when you make it past this period, because every day you will have made the choice to keep pushing through the tough times. You will have made that conscious decision to persist— no matter the end result of any individual day—despite your lack of motivation, dwindling hope, diminished support, continual mistakes, fear of failure, or any other excuse for why you couldn't go on.

I do want to quickly explain what I mean when I use the metaphor of building a structure. Building a structure doesn't mean being an entrepreneur, traveling the world, going to an Ivy League university, quitting your job, getting a corner-office corporate position, making your family proud, or anything else. It simply means living life the way that is most true to yourself. If, after reading this book and doing all of the reflecting it requires, you find that you love cutting and styling hair, then you've already got the blueprints for your structure. If nothing brings you more joy than changing oil and repairing cars, and you're doing that, then you've won. If being the best damn parent you can be is what you most desire, then do that. Building your structure is doing whatever brings you the most joy, makes you feel the most alive, and is most true to you. It's that simple.

When I claimed responsibility for my life, I was able to begin transitioning from viewing myself as the victim to being the potential victor. With that responsibility came a deep sense of remorse for the choices I had made and the people I had wronged. However, people began to see I was serious about turning my life around, and with that, I slowly regained some of the trust I had lost in my relationships.

When you go through adversity and are finally able to claim your role in it, you realize that you have two options: either regret that period of your life and wish you could do it all over, or be grateful it happened and extract every lesson that it can teach you. Like I mentioned earlier, looking back on your life is crucial, but regretting your choices is detrimental. You need to capitalize on your adversity just like it capitalized on you in your lowest point.

For me, gratitude was less like flipping a switch and more like the long, slow process of waiting for water to boil when you're really hungry. Around the same time that I was learning the importance of practicing gratitude, I noticed something that now seems to be quite obvious.

As I was busy digging my way to rock bottom, I was so consumed by substances meant to numb my pain that I failed to realize that safety nets, ropes, and other lifelines were being thrown out to help prevent me from digging deeper. It wasn't until hindsight allowed me to look to my past with clarity that I saw the number of opportunities I had to be pulled into safety. Lifelines may be one of the most important aspects of this book, because if you can notice and grab hold of them as they're thrown to you, the adversity you face has the potential to be much less severe than it otherwise may have been.

It wasn't until a lifeline was practically hand-delivered to me and tied around my waist that I was able to begin climbing back out of the hole I had dug for myself. That lifeline was the phone call about the open spot on the upcoming deployment. Important to mention is that lifelines often don't appear as such and are therefore missed because we fail to realize that they were even there for our benefit . . . until it's too late. This next chapter will help you not only notice them, but also grab hold of them so that you can regroup, set your sights on a different path, and proceed down it with a better plan.

"The reason most people don't recognize an opportunity when they meet it is because it usually goes around wearing overalls and looking like hard work."

Unknown

6

LIFELINES: THEY'LL SAVE YOU IF YOU CAN SPOT THEM

Life•line: noun
1) a thing on which someone or something depends or which provides a means of escape from a difficult situation.

—Merriam Webster Dictionary

2) a thing (such as a person, opportunity, event, or lesson) that someone desperately needs or which provides a means of escape from a difficult situation and reclaims their hope for a better future.

—Jake Widmann

I don't know how many times I wished that some magical thing was simply going to appear one day and make my life all better. Maybe a close family member would find me a great job. Maybe I would wake up one morning and finally decide to move to one of the cities I had in mind after returning home from my deployment. Maybe I would have an epiphany, life would all of a sudden make sense, and I would quit being an idiot. Maybe. Maybe. Maybe. All the hoping and wishing in the world weren't going to pull me out from the mess my life had become. But *maybe* if I had only known that a different, better path for my life was closer than I had thought, I would have been able to figure things out before taking the expressway to hell.

I should have seen that, since I was the one deconstructing my life, I should have also been the one who took responsibility for putting it back together. However, for some reason that never clicked for me. I came home from my first deployment with one thing in mind: making up for lost time by drinking and getting high with my friends for weeks on end. Then, in what seemed like no time at all, I was waking up in a jail cell, hit with the reality of my actions.

Spending my last twenty dollars at the bar was the wake-up call I needed, forcing me to begin reflecting on the choices I was making. But it wasn't until that phone call to go on my second deployment that I reclaimed a brighter hope for my future and let go of the stress and anxiety I had been carrying for months. The thing is, in the years since that phone call, I've noticed just how many opportunities prior to it I missed.

What makes lifelines so tricky is they hardly ever appear as a phone call offering you an opportunity. Oftentimes, they're only a subtle nudge; an attempt to make you stop and think about your choices. For example, when I woke up in the corner booth of the club and got fired from my job, I had an opportunity to reflect on the choices that I had made that led me to that point—a lifeline. Unfortunately, as I see so many people do, I chose to laugh it off and hope for the best going forward, failing to realize it was a prime opportunity to question the path I was traveling down.

HELP IS ALL AROUND US

I believe that, as we're going through life, a force—the universe, God, or whatever it is you believe in—is always throwing us lifeline. When a lifeline is tossed out to us, it leaves us with the responsibility of first spotting it and then deciding what to do once we see it. When that we need to grab for it, we may not be in a spot to properly utilize it. Our ability to use that lifeline to its full potential can be diminished by a severe addiction, a lack of belief in ourselves, or any other number of factors.

When we fail to notice a lifeline, it's just as useless as if it had been out of reach to begin with. It was only when I took the time to reflect on my life that I noticed how many opportunities I was given to step away from the life I was living and straighten my path. I completely squandered those opportunities because I didn't see them as such, or I didn't want to put in the work to grab them.

When I returned home from Vegas, I was literally and figuratively hungover. It took my body a week to recover from the abuse I put it through, and I'm not sure my mind even made it back to the Midwest until after the twelve days of sobriety while on house arrest. Upon returning home from Vegas, a lifeline—my feeling that I was losing control of my life—was there, waiting for me to grab it. It was within reach as I recalled the events of my nearly two-week-long trip to my friends as we sat in my living room getting high. The only thing I needed to do was grab onto it—realize I was committing to a path that clearly led to a dead end. I only needed to acknowledge the thoughts I was having that my life was getting out of control and allow them to pull me off the path I had stepped onto. Yet I joked about the trip with my friends, who replied as if I were some hero for having "lived it up" in Vegas. While telling stories of my trip high in the presence of my friends, it was easy to get caught up in the romanticized events, but during the days and weeks after, whenever I had brief flashes of sobriety I felt that there was something I was missing.

These events, like those after my return from Vegas, were frozen in my mind as if they were frames of a movie, plucked out and dropped into my long-term memory. I became curious about them because, even though many of them didn't seem all that significant, they remained as vivid as any. Possibly it was because these memories all had one common thread: I was sober.

Now, I know you're probably thinking, "Well, duh! Alcohol and weed aren't known to be the best tools to help preserve memories . . ." Yes, I certainly can't disagree with that, but these memories felt more significant than just an altruistic favor from my brain working to preserve the rare flashes of time when I was sober, usually in the wake of a night of heavy drinking. As I worked my way through this chapter, I began to see undoubtedly why those memories were significant.

They were the lifelines. They were the chances I had to right my path. They were the periods of time when I was fully aware of what I had done and was being given the opportunity to stop, think, and make better decisions going forward. They were significant, because, if only I had spotted them, my pain and suffering might have ended there, rather than many months down the road.

There were countless other people, opportunities, events, and lessons to grab hold of and pull myself into a brighter future, but most often I failed to notice them. Occasionally, when I did notice them, I couldn't hold on long enough to provide any benefit anyway. I think if you look back on your life, you too will realize there have been many lifelines you've missed.

My brother and my nephew picking me up from jail was an opportunity for me to stop and reflect on how far I had drifted from the person I envisioned myself being when I was younger.

Returning from Vegas after spending my money foolishly and disavowing every value I thought I lived by was a chance for me to stomp my foot and reevaluate where my choices were taking me.

Every individual event that caused the respect and trust of my family to be depleted could have been the proof I apparently needed to stop trying to prove to myself that I could drink responsibly.

Moving out of my apartment with my roommate and into one by myself was an opportunity for a fresh start, one where I could finally hold myself to a higher level of personal accountability and responsibility—but, again, I failed.

I registered for the spring semester at a local community college a few months after returning home because I knew it would give some structure to my life and afford me the opportunity to do something other than getting high and drinking. However, when the first day of the semester arrived, I called the school and unenrolled from classes.

Having to begin withdrawing from the 401K my mom advised me to set up should have been a fair warning that I needed to get my shit together, but I saw it as allowing myself to procrastinate a little longer until that magical opportunity I was hoping for came along.

I could go on and on, but all of these lifelines, and many others that I haven't mentioned, were available for me to take advantage of. The catch was that I had to be the one who made the decision. It's obvious now that these events should have served as warning signs, maybe even dead-end markers, but my immaturity, ignorance, know-it-all attitude, and perpetual intoxication encouraged me to keep my head down, believing that everything was okay and I was right, until I was eventually left with no option but to look up and see that I was surrounded by a desolate wasteland and I was the only inhabitant.

UNDERSTANDING YOUR STORY
WILL GIVE YOU TRUE FREEDOM

I'm well aware that going on a deployment probably isn't an option for you, nor would you likely want it to be. Each person who picks up this book will have their own way of making it through their adversity. As for you and me, we're completely different people, so we should expect that our individual solutions to a challenging period of life will be different.

Your focus should be on the overall theme of this chapter and not the specific events which helped save me on my journey. It's your life—not mine, not your friends', not anyone else's. The opportunities you have to get your life back on track are not going to be the same as the opportunities I was afforded, but I can assure you the end result will be similar.

Although deploying (again) was not the first thing I wanted to do, I knew that it was the best option I had. It's not fun or easy being away from family. It's not pleasant having guns and rockets shot at your base while you're working, lifting weights, sleeping, or eating dinner. It's not easy putting your life on hold in order to go to a foreign country for a year while everybody else's life continues back home. I made that sacrifice because I knew that I deserved a better future and that this would be a stepping stone toward it.

To ensure this step led me to a desired location, I maintained the new habits I created while on house arrest. I continued reading books that helped me further open my eyes, expand my mind, and look deep within myself. I made myself a priority. I worked diligently to repair my relationships with family and friends. I spent the first five months of my deployment essentially working for free so I could repay the debts owed to my family, the bank, the holder of the lien against my car, and elsewhere. For the first time in a long time, I put my time and energy into the things I knew would pay me dividends in the future.

The most valuable activity for me came in the form of writing a twenty-six-page memoir recounting that span of time I was home between my first and second deployments. I felt the need to be open, upfront, and honest about the life I had lived and the choices I had made. Most of what I had done was already out in the open, but there was a large part of my life that still remained a mystery to my family.

I began with a general idea of what I wanted to say. I wanted to write it for my own benefit, but I knew all along that I needed to give it to the people I'd hurt so they could hopefully gain a deeper understanding of the reasoning behind my choices and actions. The writing started out slow, and I was unsure how open and honest I wanted to be. *Should I talk about failing my urinalysis before my first deployment?* I thought. *Should I talk about blacking out every time I drank? Should I talk about the events of Vegas? Should I talk about how worthless and undeserving I feel to have a family as patient as mine?*

I wrote down the details, recalled the events, and explained my thoughts. Eventually I had something I was ready to share with my family and whomever they decided to pass it along to. I was nervous because I wouldn't be there to answer any questions as they read through it or to further justify why I'd done something. However, I knew that sending the copies I had printed off was the right thing to do. It helped me to heal and learn more about myself. I was hoping it would do the same for them.

I grabbed each stack of paper from the printer, hole-punched the top left corner, and looped some military paracord through it to bind the pages together. I took it to the post office and individually mailed out each thick stack of paper to the respective recipient. Doubt didn't arise until I was standing in that line. I wasn't sure if my family was ready for the stories each page held. What I did know was that once I took those nine months' worth of misery from my head and put them down on paper, I felt much better. Maybe they would be appalled at the decisions I'd made and never look at me the same way again. Maybe my family would never trust me again. I wasn't sure what the outcome would be, but knew that I had done the right thing for myself.

Since that first lie I told my mom upon coming back from the weekend camping trip at age fourteen, I had continued to build more and more lies of differing severity on top of it. Over the years, I found myself keeping track of so many lies, twists, and tales that every time my phone rang, my heart raced at the thought that she had discovered another lie I told. The decision to write this short memoir was what helped to absolve me of the guilt I held from the untold stories, half-truths, and outright lies told to not only my mother but to everyone for whom I had concocted a different version of the real story for in order to protect myself or a friend.

When I mailed out those bound pages, it felt like I had broken free from the shell of a life I was living. Anyone who cared to take a look would have seen the real, raw, genuine version of myself. I could finally live authentically and unrestrained by the different versions of stories I had told everyone. I could finally open up and talk freely without having to worry about what parts of the story or lies I had previously told someone. Those lies were my primary cause of unnecessary anxiety, but with the words printed out, I gave myself an infinite number of blank pages that I could use to write a better future. I dumped the constant heap of lies I towed with me everywhere onto those pages, and as quickly as you could mail a package, my anxiety was gone.

That short memoir also held me accountable to something when I returned home; I made promises—to myself, most importantly, but also to my family—that I wouldn't go back down that road again. Those promises were the guiding voice that, when I returned home and found myself in questionable situations, allowed me to ask myself, "Should I really be doing this? Is this going to get me closer to where I want to be? Who am I potentially harming by doing this?"

The deployment was the opportunity I was afforded, but I decided to use that opportunity and compound it by writing the short memoir. After I had mailed it out, the deployment continued along much as it had been. During that time, I began to realize the incredible power the relationships in our lives have. When surrounded by people who challenged and encouraged me, I was capable of great things. However, when nothing was expected of me, I lacked the drive and persistence to do anything worthwhile. This realization would fully catalyze years later, but for now, it was a step in the right direction.

RELATIONSHIPS: (CAN BE)
THE GREATEST LIFELINES

The individual days of the deployment evolved into daily routines, which helped to pass the hours more quickly. During that time, relationships with the people I was deployed with grew stronger, and I came to realize that in order to be successful upon returning home I would need to have a solid plan in place. No longer could I float through life, reacting to what my choices were inevitably handing me. I knew if I was going to stay on the right path long term, I would need to begin distancing myself from toxic relationships as well as those with people who only ever wanted to hang out if alcohol was involved— something I clearly did not need in my life.

If there were a graph where the y-axis was the number of friends I had and the x-axis was time, it would be a bell curve. We'll call it the "Friends Come and Go Graph." I honestly think this could represent most people's friendship timeline. Our childhood and teen years begins with making friends. Then we gain more friends than we could hope for. During our later years, we realize who our real friends are, so we naturally tend to those relationships. Then, through it all, we're left with a couple best friends who have seen it all, know it all, and will likely be by our side for years to come.

When I came back from my first deployment, I was the one buying shots for ten people at a time, multiple times a night. I would feed anyone who came over to my house and never ask for a dollar while they also drank the alcohol I had purchased. Then, when I started to be more conservative with how I spent my money, my "friends" started to be more conservative with how much time they hung around me. I was still the same person they appeared to be friends with; I simply wasn't buying drinks for them anymore. I learned the y-axis of the "Friends Come and Go Graph" not only correlates with time; it decreases with your money as well.

This didn't bother me until I realized that it was the come-and-go friends whom I was giving the majority of my time and energy to. Instead of spending time with family, I was hanging out with people who wouldn't have had my back when I most needed them. Instead of building a deeper connection with the two or three best friends I actually had, I was spreading my love for people so thin that I had little left to give to those who deserved it. The test to implement this knowledge would come upon arriving home, when I'd be thrown back into the same location with the same people and the same vices attempting to pull me back onto my previous path. I knew I needed to begin looking for lifelines—before I needed them—that would ensure my best chance for success.

As my deployment drew closer to an end, I began contemplating what I would do once I returned home. My friend Alex, whom I was deployed with for the second time, was going to be attending college at

The University of Wisconsin–Whitewater, about three hours south of my hometown. I vividly remembered my failed attempts to move out of my hometown last time I was home and thought that this would be the perfect opportunity.

Alex, who had struggled with some challenges similar to mine, was someone who I trusted with my life and is still a best friend. He committed to helping to keep me in line, as I would do for him, if we were to live together. I had all the faith in the world that we would make this work, so we agreed to make our talks about moving in together a reality once we returned home. I hoped that we could each serve as a lifeline for each other, helping to keep one another in line.

The final weeks of deployment passed us by, and after a few lengthy flights I was once again flying back into my little airport in central Wisconsin. I stepped back onto familiar ground with a heavy desire to never return back to where I was one short year ago, a desire fueled by months of working on myself: lifting weights, running, reading, writing, and engaging in self-reflection.

Unfortunately, the fight against the very real and underestimated power of addiction, combined with familiar faces and my return to my old environment, wouldn't be an easy battle to win. Much like after my release from jail, I found myself thrown back into a setting in which I had proven I couldn't handle myself responsibly.

> *"Don't change just to impress and please someone. Change because it makes you a better person and it leads you to a better future. When you have to start compromising yourself of your morals for the people around you, it's probably time to change the people around you."*
>
> —Unknown

SET YOURSELF UP FOR SUCCESS,
OR BE DESTINED FOR FAILURE

Within the initial couple weeks of returning home, I had already become uncomfortable with how much my life was resembling my return home from my first deployment. Granted, there were no two-week trips to Vegas, but I had gotten high and drunk multiple times, just not at the same alarming rate as before. I was able to curb my obnoxious blacking out, but as two weeks turned into a month, I was slowly increasing the frequency and the intensity of my drinking and smoking weed.

It goes to show that sometimes we need more than only a will to change. Upon returning home from Afghanistan, my will to change was there. Heck, I told my family in no less than a couple dozen pages exactly what they could expect from me going forward. Yet here I was, a month into being home. Just like after getting out of jail and returning to drinking, I was resorting to the same old same old when faced with the question, "To drink, or not to drink?" They say history tends to repeat itself, and while I had always believed that to be true, I never thought it would circle back around this quickly or with such a vengeance for my ability to make responsible decisions.

Sometimes we need to forcibly remove ourselves from the situation in order to make the changes we desire. I had begun making a few trips to Whitewater to look for apartments with Alex and to break free from the routine I was creating. I had returned home after a few days only to turn right back around to go stay with Alex's family after pulling the final straw for my mom, whose house I was staying at back home. Apparently two cops knocking on her door to escort my mostly unconscious body to her house wasn't what she envisioned when I promised her, and the rest of my family, that I would be turning my life around when I got back home.

The night began at a friend's house to pregame and wait for everyone to gather before going out to the bars. I've never been too good at pregaming, as I usually treated it like all other drinking: pounding beers and anything else within arm's reach. It only took an hour or two after arriving at the bar before I was thrown out of it. Apparently I had bumped into a guy and spilled his drink, and he wasn't too fond of that. He proceeded to grab hold of my throat and press my head against the top of the bar. Friends came to my rescue—and so did the bouncer, only to kick me out.

I began walking the six miles to my brother's house, but was distracted by a group of people at about the first mile. They were getting high on an apartment stoop, and I proceeded to make friends with them and let them get me high too. I took a few hits from their pipe and then proceeded to accidentally drop it on the ground. In a short time, I felt remarkably higher than I had ever been. I hung around for a while longer until wandering my way onto . . .

◘

I woke the next morning in a familiar location, but was confused about how I had gotten there. I made my way downstairs to the kitchen of my mom's house, where she had been awaiting my presence. I could tell that I was about to walk into a war zone, and the only thing I could do was sit there and listen to my mother tell me about whatever had happened last night.

"Jake, you have literally no idea what it's like to be woken up in the middle of the night by two officers knocking on your door informing you they found your child lying facedown in the hospital parking lot. I've had to dread that moment for years now because you can't get your shit together. I thought that worst nightmare had finally come true last night," my mom said.

"You're right. I don't." I wasn't sure what else to say.

"I can't do this anymore. I have too much going on right now. I can't be worrying every night whether or not you're lying dead somewhere. You're no longer allowed to stay here." She walked out of the house and slammed the door behind her.

I slid my feet into my shoes, walked down the driveway, and waved goodbye to my stepdad, who was mowing the lawn. My phone was dead, so the only option left was to trek about ten miles to my friend's house where my car was parked. My walk, with periods of jogging, consisted of profanity-filled phrases directed at myself for my lack of ability, yet again, to be a responsible human. I had made it about three miles before Chris, the friend whose house my car was parked at, picked me up to give me a ride to my vehicle.

Chris dropped me off at my car, and I drove to my dad's house to spend the rest of the day there. It was somewhere I always felt a little more at ease, not judged for the perpetually stupid decisions I seemed to be incapable of escaping. He's a good listener, and he always ended our conversations by letting me know that, while he might not approve of my actions, he would always be there for me. I spent a little while longer at my dad's, ate lunch, and then called Alex, the friend I would be getting an apartment with, to ask if I could stay with him.

I left my dad's and drove to live with Alex until we found an apartment in Whitewater. Over the next month, I spent a majority of my time away from home. I knew that I had little self-control to commit to the promises I had made to myself and others while overseas. Although Alex and I were drinking more than we had agreed to before returning home, we excused it with the idea that once we moved into the apartment, which we had recently signed a lease on, we would be hitting the gym and getting our routine dialed in.

It sure didn't seem like it then, but getting kicked out of my mom's house was a lifeline, because it allowed me to more easily distance myself from the disastrous recipe of people, surroundings, activities, and, ultimately, choices that were continually leading me to undesired destinations. I could tell that I had changed from whom I was roughly a year or two ago. In the past, I knew that my choices were making me infinitely more miserable, but I still couldn't bring myself to make the changes I knew I needed to make. It's something that, in years since, I've seen many others struggle with as well. Oftentimes it's not a lack of knowledge or even a lack of awareness of a problem, but simply a lack of just doing it.

I suppose part of the issue is the whole "analysis paralysis" cycle that often accompanies the twenty-something stage of life. It's a point of many crossroads, where every possible option is (over)analyzed until we run out of time and choose something we aren't too enthusiastic about, we choose nothing at all and maintain our status quo, or we run out of resources and get funneled into a path we also aren't too enthusiastic about. For me, it was the latter.

LIFE CAN SEEM TO FALL APART IN SECONDS, BUT IT CAN ALSO SEEM TO COME TOGETHER IN SECONDS

Over that next month, I took a few trips home to see family and take care of miscellaneous things. Other than that, I remained focused on my goal of limiting or eliminating contact with people who I thought would lead my new life to resemble anything close to my past. I had been home from my deployment for nearly two months now. I had some small goals set for the upcoming semester and was looking forward to living a mostly "normal" life while I focused on school.

I think there are several moments in everyone's life when they have made enough small steps that it becomes possible to have a mindset shift, a realization—an epiphany, so to speak—that forces them to look at some aspect of their lives differently. I hope, if anything, this book leads you to a few of those and that they allow you to live a more fruitful life. For me, this was after I had finally made enough awful decisions that I was able to feel the desire to change my life deep within me. I was done dancing on the bar, passing out in unpredictable places, and being the life of the party. I had done enough "living" over the past years and was ready to settle into the actual responsibilities of adulthood and stop acting like a college student.

The day had come for Alex and me to move into our apartment. I made a short trip back home to load my belongings onto a trailer. Aside from moving, I also wanted to catch up with a friend I hadn't yet been able to meet up with since being home. I arrived in my hometown early in the afternoon and dropped in to surprise her where she worked.

I placed my car in park a few spots back from her store, a tanning salon, and walked up to the front door. I opened the door and expected to surprise Haley with a loud and excited, "Heyyy!"—but I was the one who was surprised. A beautiful girl with brownish-blonde hair and beaming blue eyes, roughly the same age as Haley, was sitting at the desk. Normally, a jumble of words would have fallen from my mouth before I realized it would be wise to cut my losses and awkwardly say goodbye. But this time, I grabbed a seat in the wicker chair in front of the big picture window and carried on a casual conversation for the next few minutes. We chatted about our plans for the upcoming week-end and our individual summers, and I played with her dog while she and I filled in the occasional silence with some small talk.

To my surprise, I was actually able to talk to this attractive woman, whose name was Brittany, without sweating nervously or being obnox-iously intoxicated. We talked long enough for me to be certain that I wanted to know more about her. However, I could tell that she had to get back to work. Since it was a tanning salon, and I was already there, I decided to go tanning.

To this day, Brittany still believes—or, at the very least, likes to tell people—that I specifically came into that store to go tanning. However, that's just not true. Believe who you want, but the fact is that I did go tanning (so judge me if you please). After the fifteen minutes I was in there, I got out and left—without getting her number. Idiot. Luckily, she added me on Facebook within an hour or two of me leaving. Within that first week, I asked her to go on a date when I eventually made it back home again.

After a few weeks had passed, I couldn't help but create an excuse in order to go home for that date. From that first date forward we spent almost every day of the next month together: going to the beach, having campfires, going for walks—normal summer activities. For the first time since I was probably fourteen or fifteen years old, I had my eyes opened up to the fact that alcohol wasn't a prerequisite to having fun. I had more fun in that month than I had throughout any in my recent past, and I earned back enough of my family's trust that my mom allowed me to sleep at her house while I was back home from Whitewater.

The new excitement surrounding this new ability to have fun without drinking was . . . intoxicating—pun intended. Prior to meeting Brittany, Alex and I were still drinking more than I wanted to, so I found every reason I could to stay back in my hometown to spend more time with Brittany. I was paying rent while mostly living back home for the first month of mine and Alex's lease, but the deep commitment to changing my life wasn't a joke, and I felt that I was traveling further and faster down the right path than ever before in my adult life.

On one random afternoon, a stop to see a friend had serendipitously turned into meeting a woman who, in one month, helped me take more steps toward the future I desired than I had made over the past two or three years. I could wake up early in the morning without a hangover and, before getting out of bed, text Brittany to see what her plans were for the day. We would spend the entire day together and didn't need to consume a drop of alcohol to make life more enjoyable.

I became addicted to the feeling of earning back my family's trust. It felt good hearing my parents tell me they could notice I had changed and that they were glad I was back. I would contest, however, that I wasn't back. I was someone different altogether. For two years, I had been fighting to get back to the old Jake, that previous version of who I used to be. While most of that previous version had finally been restored, I had also gained many other positive traits that I'd never had before. It wasn't just the return of a previous version of myself; it was the beginning of a new, better, more aware version.

Spending time with Brittany brought out the best in me. It brought out the best parts of who I was at the core, who I wanted to be and was fighting to get to while drudging through hell. It was Brittany who I thought of when I left a party after only an hour to walk back to my friend's house and fall asleep on his couch. "Old Jake" didn't leave parties to fall asleep. At least, not intentionally. Old Jake either passed out with near alcohol poisoning or shut things down at the end of the night. It was her who I thought of when I was offered weed and said no.

It was these changes within me that led me to tell Alex that I wasn't happy with the amount we had been drinking while living together in Whitewater. We hadn't kept our promises to hold each other accountable, and I knew that returning home to be closer to family and Brittany was the right choice. I packed up and drove three hours back home after having lived in Whitewater for only three months.

Sometimes you have to make decisions that appear absolutely ludicrous but that you know deep down are correct. This was one of those decisions. I had reached a point where I was committed to changing my life for good, and nothing—even the plans I made with one of my best friends—was going to stop me. I couldn't easily afford the lease I had on the apartment, which I still had to pay five months of, but I knew that I had to make it work.

I had grabbed hold of a lifeline that was moving me closer to the life I desired than anything I had managed to do on my own. I had someone else to devote my time to and a renewed outlook on life, where alcohol wasn't the central theme.

I obviously can't promise that a beautiful lady or a gorgeous man is going to come into your life and help you transition through your adversity. What I can promise is that, if you keep your eyes open for these profound new things we're calling lifelines, the journey to where you want to be will consist of substantially fewer roadblocks and detours.

A lifeline, as you've seen, can be anything that your unique self can utilize to make it past a rough patch of life. What I prefer, however, is to perform a regular audit of my life. Meaning, while I'm going down the path I'm on, I take time to reflect, assess goals, determine if I'm straying from them, and then readjust. By doing this, I never stray more than a few steps from the path I've chosen for myself, and the need for lifelines is almost nonexistent.

"We lie loudest
when we lie
to ourselves."

Eric Hoffer

7

WE NEED TO STOP
LYING TO OURSELVES

I want to take a few steps back—back to my second deployment once again. I'm doing it this way because a lot happened around the time of my second deployment, and to properly and accurately lay it out for you, I need to hit rewind. Lifelines are those opportunities available to us in times of adversity. But what if there were a way to avoid some of that adversity, or possibly minimize its effects before it got out of hand? Well, I believe there is. I've found that so many people lie to themselves on a daily basis, and if we could cut this lie from our lives, I truly believe that it would be possible to bypass much of our adversity—not entirely, but we could certainly shorten our journey through it. I would guess that you've had this thought at some point (and if you haven't said it, or even thought it, then I guarantee that you've subconsciously believed it): "It will never be me, until . . ."

My ankle bracelets were proof against the subconscious belief that I held onto for years: *I won't get caught. It will never be me . . .* Clearly they were lies I had to tell myself to be okay with the choices I was making. Nevertheless, my ankle bracelets had been removed and I was over a month into training with my unit before deploying overseas.

Weeks passed, and soon we had landed in Bagram, Afghanistan, after roughly twenty-four hours of flying from the East Coast to this foreign country in southern Asia.

The heat was intense. The task of settling into a new "home" had begun, and in the moment the only thing my fellow soldiers and I wanted to do was sleep. All of the tents were filled with other service members transitioning in and out of the country, so we did the next best thing: we dropped our bags on the sand and rocky ground and laid on top of them to sleep in the brightly lit area. It was already past midnight, and ahead of us was a long day of travel to our final destination.

I closed my eyes and, after the occasional peek to see what everyone was doing, was on my way to falling asleep in minutes. The busy base was covered in noise, from massive military planes and jets utilizing the nearby runway to heavy machinery operating in the vicinity and other soldiers roaming about the area. A day of travel on a cramped airplane lugging around three or four bags was all the sleep aid I needed to quickly pass out. The sound of jets, machinery, and random passersby quickly became methodical and almost soothing. But then one noise, different from the rest, interrupted our sleep: a siren.

We immediately carried out the training we had received prior to deploying. We picked up our weapons and ran toward the nearest cement bunker that wasn't already filled with people seeking safety from the incoming mortars or rockets. The sound of sirens was mixed with yells of "Incoming!" and the scattering of rocks beneath people's feet as they ran in every direction. It was like turning over an old, decayed log in the woods and watching as the hundreds of previously unsuspecting bugs beneath it scrambled to seek refuge.

My heart raced as I made it to the bunker and looked around to see who from my unit was with me. I was half confused, still disoriented from having just woken up, and half in disbelief, realizing that the training we had gone through wasn't just precautionary—it was necessary. As I sat under the bunker crammed full of other soldiers, I looked across the rocky landscape, seeing all the other bunkers filled with soldiers as well. While the people in my unit were caught off guard and still trying to wake up, the soldiers who had been there a while were joking around, hanging halfway out of the bunkers as though it would never be them who were hurt or killed.

It was a scene I didn't expect to see. I suppose that seems a bit odd to hear from me, someone who gambled with his life and everyone else's on the road each time he got into the car and decided to drive drunk. But this seemed more real, and the effects seemed more devastating. The whistling sound of rockets as they flew overhead and the earth shaking as they crashed into the ground were, no pun intended, sobering. It wasn't something I expected people to take lightly. Some soldiers stood out in the open air smoking a cigarette, joking around, and blowing off the very solid reality of the situation.

Then again, I'd just had my ankle bracelets removed the day before reporting to my unit for training. Wasn't I essentially one of them, albeit under different circumstances? Were my actions of getting behind the wheel at varying levels of intoxication any different than their choice to stand outside the cement bunkers?

This scene made me look at the risks we take in life a bit differently. Risks are an inescapable part of life. We tremble at the thought of risking money, time, sleep, or comfort on a better future, a business opportunity, an investment, helping a friend or stranger, or stepping outside our comfort zone. However, all too often we take risks that offer no reward and instead come with heavy consequences.

Instead, many of us take our risks on the very things we know we shouldn't be doing. I'm guessing you're one of them, or you probably wouldn't still be reading this book. We take these risks knowing somewhere deep down within ourselves that the thought in the back of our minds, *It'll never be me,* only serves to comfort us until next time . . . which always eventually turns into out of time.

I IMAGINE WE'RE ALL LYING
(TO OURSELVES) ABOUT SOMETHING

Think back to the last time you did something significant that you know you shouldn't have done: drank and drove, cheated, hit a parked car without saying anything, did drugs, excessively gambled, smoked cigarettes, lied, stole, or spent two hours on Facebook when you only went on to "check notifications." What thoughts crossed your mind as you fumbled to put your keys in the ignition to drive home, as you lied to your spouse about where you were, as you drove away from the person's vehicle you just hit, got high, blew your entire paycheck, smoked two packs a day, told that lie, stuffed that shirt into your backpack, or woke up tired the next morning because you stayed up too late scrolling your news feed?

Did you possibly think to yourself, "It'll never be me," "I won't get caught this time," or "I don't have a problem"? I couldn't come close to recalling how many times I've told myself that. But here's the thing: we don't actually need to say or think it at all. Anytime we engage in activities like these, it's what we subconsciously believe, whether or not we acknowledge the consequences of getting caught. We would never do them if we knew, or even thought, that this was the day we'd get caught, become homeless, get hurt, hurt someone else, be diagnosed with lung cancer, or go broke.

Our denial of the potential—or, should I say, inevitable—consequences motivates us to make our ill-advised decisions. Denial, at least in a psychological sense, is the failure to acknowledge an unacceptable truth or emotion or to admit it into consciousness. We use it as a defense mechanism.

Denial was my middle name. I had driven while blackout drunk countless times. I had passed out in bars, streets, sidewalks, parking lots, lawns, restaurants, strangers' houses, and dance club floors. After months of excessive drinking, I had developed unbearable heartburn. I would go days without being able to eat much of anything at all, but it didn't stop me from drinking. In my infinite wisdom, I chose to handle it by alternating drinking from a bottle of Pepto-Bismol and a beer. Genius, right? I have been permanently banned from a dozen or more bars. I got a misdemeanor for fleeing an officer, paid fines, did jail time, and got a DUI. I had done all of this and more, and I still couldn't admit that alcohol was a serious problem in my life.

Instead of owning up to the truth, we regularly run from it. Hearing the truth means that we have to step outside our comfort zone and put in the hard work to solve the problems that we created. It took me years to admit that I was an alcoholic. I would sugarcoat it by saying, "I just can't drink Jack Daniels." Then, I realized that that wasn't the entire truth, and I began saying, "I just can't drink hard liquor." That form of denial later transitioned into, "Okay, maybe I have a little drinking problem." Eventually, with the help of Brittany, a counselor, and many failed attempts at trying to mask my alcoholism with socially acceptable words and phrases, I finally gave into the fact that I was indeed (dun-dun-duuuun) an alcoholic.

However, I've found that we all, or at least the vast majority of us, do this to some extent, in our own unique way. Just swap out alcoholism with your chosen form of addiction: food, awful relationships, drugs, your cell phone, money, sex, prescriptions, gambling, low self-confidence, or perfection.

Ultimately, I was a coward for not facing my problems and dealing with them, but I wouldn't be writing this book if I didn't feel like people needed help making those changes while also using the lessons they learn to create a meaningful life.

I know that I can get you to admit this journey is not an easy one. It's anything but easy. You have to really want the dreams you once held onto so adamantly. You have to want to put your problems behind you. You have to know that eventually, with enough effort and development of new routines, you can have the life you desire. It starts with accepting that you got yourself into this position. Denying the reasons you are where you are is only ever going to keep you there.

CLOSE ONLY COUNTS IN HORSESHOES
AND (ROCKET-PROPELLED) GRENADES

My gaze was focused on the soldiers standing out in the open, well within range of the incoming bombs. I thought, *How dumb could you be? The base is being bombed, and you're going to joke around in the open, unprotected air?* The thought may not have ever crossed their minds, but their actions spoke clearly. They had become fully accustomed to the regular sound of the sirens and the nearby crashing of bombs that fear no longer motivated them to take cover.

What does this stand to teach you and me? Can we simply rephrase the statement into, "It may happen to me," or "It will eventually happen to me"? Could that slight change in wording be the simple mindset shift we need to prevent us from making irrational decisions? Would that make us stop, even if only for a second, and think about the choices that we were about to make? In the case of your well-being, your hopes and dreams, your future, and your life, that second might be the most important one. Are you going to press your luck or commit to changing?

The base intercom system let us know the threat was no longer present, and the frenzy came to an end. We meandered back to our bags. A few people went back to sleep. I made my way with a few other soldiers to the dining facility for an early morning snack. Sleep wasn't on my mind anymore.

Later that morning, we assembled by the airstrip to fly via helicopter to our new home for the next nine months. The hourlong flight over the Afghan landscape was surprisingly impressive. The landscape in Kuwait is flat and covered in gray and yellowish sand, and the air appears to be visibly toxic. Afghanistan, at least from a height of a couple thousand feet, was scattered with patches of lush farmland, a river or stream here and there, and beautiful, rugged, rocky mountains with cities containing buildings no more than a few stories tall scattered about the land. There was still an abundance of sand, but the varying terrain and a temperature less than 130 degrees (unlike that which plagues Kuwait) were a pleasant surprise. The helicopter zipped over a large city and, shortly after, touched down just off of the long runway stretching the length of the base.

It didn't take longer than a few weeks to settle into our lodgings, which mostly consisted of nothing more than plywood that shook every time a plane or helicopter flew within its vicinity.

The highlights of our days included completing our duties within the office, working out in the gym, and either calling home to family, reading a book, watching movies, or playing video games. We were a finance unit, so our main job was to disburse cash to soldiers and vendors on the base and in the local area. We also worked to resolve soldiers' pay issues, and we traveled to outlying forward operating bases to support the financial needs of those soldiers. It was far from what was shown in commercials, kicking in doors and rappelling out of helicopters, but it was a rewarding and important job nonetheless.

Creating a consistent routine is key to making it through a deployment and making the days go by quicker. Wake up, go to work, go to the gym, watch a movie, sleep. Obviously add in some time for food and hygiene, and you have a basic routine to get you through a deployment with your sanity.

Months went by, and we received, on average, a bombing every other week. It became something to be expected. I wasn't complacent enough to stand outside of a bunker as if I were bomb-resistant, like the soldiers I had witnessed months prior; however, after going through roughly a dozen attacks, I could understand their thinking.

My routine of going to the gym nearly every day began to elicit results. I suppose that's the purpose of a routine; to build upon the work of the day before. Consistency and persistence, showing up day after day, are key to achieving the results you want. Unfortunately, this bit of advice isn't something that only I knew. Apparently the enemy had caught onto the idea of consistency and persistence as well.

The sirens went off. "Incoming!" yelled people inside the weight room as they scrambled out the doors. "Go, go!" I helped my friend off the weight machine and took off running, weaving between the benches, machines, and free weights scattered about the gym. I looked back to ensure the friends I was spotting on the weight machine moments ago were still close by.

"There's a bunker over there!" someone yelled toward the dozens of people who had just poured out of the gym in search of safety from the barrage of incoming mortar shells. I could hear explosions over the whine of the siren.

"Quick, get in here and away from the ends of the bunker!" a man yelled as he motioned us inward. The rocks we were standing on trembled from the drumming of bombs into the ground.

I and the three guys I was with were all safely resting against the wall of the cement bunker. We tried to tally up how many bombs had hit the base so far. "I'd have to say at least a dozen," a guy's voice said from near the end of the bunker. "Yeah, at least that many," another said. The sirens on the base had been blaring for several minutes now. Helicopters were taking off, one after another, to seek out the enemy in hopes of eliminating or at least suppressing them.

Even after the bombing stopped, we were required to remain in the bunkers until the all-clear had been issued. The quick-reaction force performed their security checks to ensure everyone was safe and that no enemy forces had breached the perimeter. After an hour of alternating between leaning against the wall of the bunker and sitting down, the all-clear was given. The unexpected shower of enemy mortar strikes and rocket launches had killed our motivation to work out. We showered and walked to the dining facility.

At dinner we talked about the surprising number of bombs and the good fortune that no one had been hurt or killed. Nevertheless, it definitely forced us to face reality and realize that any one of the twentyish bombs that had rained down onto our base could have taken us out. After dinner, we went back to our individual rooms; from there on it was back to normal, just another day escaping death by an unknowably thin margin.

I suppose that's necessary, though. Would it be beneficial or practical for humans to focus on the things that could go wrong every second of the day? Where does the line get drawn between necessary worry and careless ignorance? If we focused on all of the things that could go wrong, we'd sit inside our houses and rock back and forth due to overwhelming anxiety.

Where I believe it becomes clearly dangerous, not only to ourselves but to those around us as well, is when an event or action fails to evoke an emotion or reaction from us. When we become desensitized, we have reached a dangerous place. When I stopped thinking that driving drunk was a risky activity and began looking at it as something that was bound to happen whenever I wanted to leave a party, I had reached a dangerous place. Drinking and driving was normal for me. I never felt the need to call my family for a ride because I was certain that it'd never be me.

HEAR NO PROBLEMS, SEE NO PROBLEMS, SPEAK OF NO PROBLEMS; HOPE FOR THE BEST

My heart beat a bit faster as I lay awake in my bed that night. There were many nights throughout that deployment that I thought about the chances of a rocket crashing through the plywood roof of the building where I and five other soldiers slept. Often, I fell asleep listening to Matchbox 20 or Blackmill, which helped to drown out the noise of the aircraft on the very nearby runway or silence the thoughts of knowing that I could potentially be closing my eyes for the last time.

The thought of any day being my last has never sat well with me. To this day, that thought terrifies me. Fortunately, while I'm in the comfort of my own home in the US, it doesn't cross my mind as often. However, when that thought was being regularly forced into my consciousness, it often made sleep hard to come by. My thoughts kept me awake just as they had when I was back home wondering how and when I was going to turn my life around. The music, much like the alcohol and weed, helped to quiet my mind. Clearly one way of dealing with the difficult thoughts was better than the other.

Throughout the nine months we spent in Afghanistan, we were bombed regularly, but rarely was it as intense as in as in the story I just shared. The bombs often landed in an area away from people and equipment. There were a few close calls with people on the base, and once they did hit a helicopter on the runway. Overall, their distant lobs in the general vicinity of our base only served to let us know that they were present and we weren't welcome.

I remembered thinking on that first night, *Those guys are crazy to be standing outside of the bunker.* Yet here I was, several months later, understanding why they did it and treating the same event with diminishing seriousness myself. When life gives us extra chances—when we get away without being dealt the consequences of our actions—we shouldn't then inch closer to the edge of the cliff, peer down toward rock bottom, and "live life on the edge." Rather, that extra chance should serve as a lifeline that we'll hopefully utilize before it's too late.

After enough extra chances, we become desensitized to the fact that our actions still have consequences. Desensitization and ignorance are easy. Awareness and action are difficult. I believe that we all want to solve problems, do big things, and overcome adversity—but when we feel a problem has become too difficult to overcome, we do nothing.

So what's a person to do? In my experience, there are only two options. We can sort of want something and then, when it gets too difficult, give up and hope that it eventually resolves itself. (It won't.) Or we can fight for the thing like our lives depend on it, because they often do. Whether or not we consciously think *It'll never be me,* choosing that first option will ensure it will eventually be you.

WHAT WILL YOU DO WHEN REALITY
KNOCKS ON YOUR DOOR?

We had roughly a month left of our deployment. We were finishing up our last missions to the outlying bases before the unit replacing us showed up and began assuming responsibility for the mission. This was an interesting time of the deployment—excitement was high, but so was complacency. Our minds were focused on our plans for when we returned and on how much we missed home, but the dangers that were relevant when we first arrived remained relevant as we were leaving.

Finally, the time for my final mission had come. The soldier I would be traveling with, Evan, and I were getting ready to head out. We were fully dressed in our combat gear. I had a backpack with a laptop and other miscellaneous items in it, and Evan had a backpack filled with roughly $80,000 worth of US and Afghan currency. We took a bus to the helipad, loaded onto the helicopter, and after a thirty-minute flight landed at the base where our mission was taking place.

This base was similar to all the others we had visited throughout our deployment. It was small, surrounded by a barrier of some sort, and littered with buildings. We set up our office, did the necessary work, and at the end of the day grabbed some dinner before going back to our room to relax. We would be sleeping in a wooden building with no interior walls. There were six cots scattered throughout it and a patchwork tin roof over our heads. We got in bed and laid awake for an hour until our conversation slowly dwindled down and we fell asleep.

When we woke up the next morning, we would be jumping on a helicopter to fly back to our base and officially closing out our last mission. The green cots we fell asleep on were anything but comfortable, but at the end of a long day and in an air-conditioned room, away from the Afghanistan heat, sleep was easier to come by. Aside from the occasional semi-conscious scramble to the nearest porta-potty, I could easily sleep throughout the night.

That is, until the explosion. The sound of rocks and rubble being thrown onto our metal roof jolted me from my bed. I instinctively grabbed my rifle and protective gear while simultaneously looking to Evan to ensure he was okay.

"Oh, shit! Get up! Get to the bunker!" Evan and I said to each other, scrambling to gather our gear. We ran to the nearest bunker, which luckily was just outside our door. We knelt down in the center next to two other people. A few more settled in over the next minute or two. "What the hell? That sounded like it hit our roof . . . did it?" Evan asked.

"I don't know, man, but it was damn close," I replied with my heart racing. "There were rocks or shrapnel hitting our roof, but it sound-ed like it hit right on top of it," I clarified to the other people in our bunker.

People were yelling around the base and scrambling to prepare for a potential attack beyond the initial one-off rocket. Someone came over to our bunker and asked if we were all okay. We explained our story and he informed us that it had hit the guard tower a few yards away. The soldier inside was concussed and would need medical attention. After another hour, we were given the all-clear and allowed to go back to our rooms to attempt to fall asleep. Unlike most nights, where we wished we could sleep for days just to pass the time quicker, on this night our only wish was for morning to arrive quicker. The reality of how close it hit was unsettling, and we were ready to welcome the apparent safety that came with daylight. In the morning, we happily strapped into the helicopter and flew back to our base.

After we got back, we shared the story with the people in our unit. We explained the details, closed out our day of business, and then went back to our rooms to pass out. The details came out over the next few days, and we were surprised to find out that the rocket was shot from nearly ten miles away. It meant nothing to me at the time, other than how lucky of a shot that was—but now, as I sit here and reflect on this story, I find it interesting just how relevant it is to my life in the year prior to coming on the deployment.

"Although the world is full of suffering, it is also full of the overcoming of it."

—Helen Keller

SOMETIMES THINGS ONLY MAKE SENSE AFTER WE'VE GROWN ENOUGH

In that year prior to this deployment, I made decisions almost daily that seemed harmless. Each day, in a vacuum, wasn't all that harmful. A day of getting drunk, possibly blacking out—so what? It happens. A breakfast consisting of leftover birthday cake and donuts isn't going to ruin your diet by itself. Telling a small lie to a family member isn't going to directly send one's life spiraling out of control. Spending a few hours in the casino occasionally isn't ruining anyone's retirement plans. We all have our escapisms, our guilty pleasures, our occasional times to let loose. Each event on its own isn't ruining anyone's life.

The thing is, when you take each of the small, unnoticeable steps and lump them all together, you're no longer talking about an innocent drunken night, a little white lie, a cheat day, or a few pulls of the slot machine's handle. It becomes something much bigger. Something that, as you learned in the chapters prior, can derail your entire life and all the big plans, hopes, and dreams you had for yourself.

After my DUI and fleeing arrest, I often thought to myself, *If only I had stayed home instead of going back to the bar for those shots, I never would have been caught,* or, *If only I hadn't gone out for dinner and a drink, I wouldn't have spent my last twenty dollars.* The thing is, we could look back over our lives and, at any undesirable turnout, say, "If only I didn't do that, or that didn't happen, then I wouldn't be where I am today." Yes, that certainly is true; however, it doesn't fix the root cause. Holding onto that truth only prolongs the inevitable. The "if only" belief only serves to make us feel good because we can fantasize about how life would be if it weren't for that single event.

The thing we overlook is the reality of the rest of the story. Nothing was going to change if weren't eventually dealt the consequences of our actions, because we could essentially go on happily believing, It'll never be me.

Those "if only" fantasies are fun to dream about, but the reality is that—whether or not I took that second trip back to the bar, and whether or not I went out for dinner and a drink that night—I would've eventually found myself in a similar spot. Those were the crucial moments of my already crumbling life, and that's why they're memorable. However, it was every single choice I made before those events that led me to make the choice that landed me there. If I hadn't gotten caught drinking and driving that night, maybe it would have happened the following weekend, the following year, or ten years after that, possibly with a much worse outcome. If I hadn't spent that last twenty, maybe I would have made it another week living the way I was, but I would've eventually found myself sitting somewhere with my head in my hands wondering how I got there.

It's never about the event itself. It's always about the journey that brought us to the event that made it possible, whether good or bad. No one wakes up one morning and decides to get addicted to crack or heroin. No one sets a goal to become an alcoholic, to gain a hundred pounds, or to become a pathological liar. The answers lie in the journey, not in one-off events that nudge us over the edge or push us toward success.

It was this realization that made me look at the rocket that threw debris onto our roof a bit differently. *Ten miles . . . huh?* I thought to myself. If the rocket went a little bit further, or the person launching it were standing a little higher up in the mountain, or the guard tower weren't there, it could have come crashing right through our thin metal roof, and I never would have known it. The next step for me would have been being boxed up and shipped back to the US with an American flag draped over my casket. There were several dozen rockets I had experienced before that one; most were only close enough to hear, and a few close enough to feel the impact, but that's about it. It was the kind of event that makes you stop and think about life itself. It makes the shift from *It'll never be me* to *It'll eventually be me quite easy.*

The rocket hitting the tower, just like the DUI and spending my last twenty dollars, was an event like every other one before it. Sure, the explosions still caused my heart to race and fear to show itself, but I had seen and heard enough bombs that they had mostly become a nuisance. After a few dozen times of drinking and driving, it became second nature. I can't begin to count how many times I woke up after a night of drinking, only to look in my wallet or check my bank account and see I had spent hundreds of dollars the night before, leaving me with enough money to get gas and two breakfast burritos from Mc-Donald's until I got paid.

Hopefully this chapter can serve as a wake-up call to the lies you may be telling yourself. And if not that, then the previous chapter will help you spot a lifeline that will pull you from the undesirable path you're on. In case you haven't realized, you don't need to be pushed from the ledge and into rock bottom before you can start making better choices. Better choices can be made right now, while you're still ahead of everyone who let themselves get too close to the edge and fell all the way down, like me.

Take time to think about that—you don't have to hit rock bottom before your life gets better. You have all the permission you need right now to begin making better choices. You can't deny the simple fact of life: you're not immune to the consequences of your actions. Eventually, that last grain of sand falls through the hourglass or that last petal falls from the rose, and, when that happens, you will be forced to face the consequences of your actions.

If there's one thing you should know, it's that what got you to where you are right now were many small, unnoticeable choices that slowly eroded the life you wanted to live. Those small, unnoticeable choices that got you here are the proof you need that small, unnoticeable, hard choices are what will get you to where you want to be.

When someone is successful, we like to think they came up overnight. "Overnight success" is a myth just as ridiculous as "overnight rock bottom." Success is only found through years and years of practice, failure, and experimentation until mastery, or a version of it, can be earned. Similarly, rock bottom is only found through years and years of actions out of alignment with one's true self, goals, and desires until a point of utter despair or total depletion of resources has been met.

Why is it, then, that we humans like to associate successes and downfalls with a single event? Because it's easy. It's the same reason we like to group, categorize, and label people. It makes our world, composed of an infinite number of grays, more black and white. However, just because it makes it easier doesn't mean it's right or beneficial. I could've much more easily made a Facebook status or blog post about the things I write about in this book, but it hardly would have made as much of an impact. Instead, I chose to write an entire book that goes in depth about my experiences and lessons learned so that you might be able to extract some of it to use on your journey.

I also get that it's hard not to compare your life and your journey to others'. The reality is that your story is yours, and my story is mine. You may be able to overcome a scenario worse than mine in half the time it took me, but it could also take you twice as long. The time it takes you to overcome your adversity will not matter once your journey begins, because you'll be focused on taking that next small step—hopefully in the right direction.

Whether your journey to rock bottom continues from here or you're ready to start the climb out, I would love for you to do one thing: don't be so hard on yourself. We're already hard enough on ourselves, and we face enough judgment from everybody else in the world as it is. Trust the journey. Do your best to make the right choices that will begin or continue your journey on the correct path. If you slip up, know that tomorrow morning is a new day to make better decisions. However, it's up to you if you'll begin making better decisions or continue along the same path you've been on.

"You are the average of the five people you spend the most time with."

_____

Jim Rohn

8

THE UPHILL BATTLE TO GET DOWNHILL MOMENTUM

All right, where were we? I went on my second deployment. I wrote a short memoir. I encountered a rocket attack closer than any I ever thought I would encounter. I returned home excited to follow through on my plans but had some significant steps down the wrong path. I met Brittany. After realizing that living with one of my best friends, Alex, wasn't going to work out, I had moved back home.

That quick summary places us near the end of 2013. September, to be exact.

◻

Something I didn't realize until later in my twenties is that staying on the right path is a perpetually challenging journey. Outside forces constantly try to pull us onto their path, stagnating our plans. My plans to get my life together once I returned home from my second deployment were, as you've read, stifled. Fortunately, my determination and a pretty girl named Brittany helped me remain persistent on that path to a better life.

I had completed the move back home from Whitewater and registered last-minute for a semester at a local university. I cruised through the semester, and by the end of it Brittany and I had plans to move to Indianapolis so I could take a job there. Before moving to Indiana, I had one final thing to follow through on: proposing to Brittany.

The move to Indiana came with what seemed like endless excitement, as Brittany and I were a newly engaged couple with our whole lives together ahead of us. However, that endless excitement came with many unforeseen challenges: challenges of communication, judgment from friends and family, financial issues, a surprise pregnancy, an unfortunate miscarriage, and, as always, life in general.

These challenges and many others prompted us to cancel our wedding, forfeiting thousands of dollars in vendor deposits. We informed our bridal party—ten on each side—and chose to do what we saw to be the right thing: refunding them the deposits for their dresses and tuxes. Goodbye, money!

It was during those difficult times that I felt I needed to get away, de-stress a little, and have some alone time. I'd tell Britt that I was going on a bike ride, and I would ride my bike two miles down the road to the pub, where I would sit for roughly an hour to enjoy a few beers and the company of the bartender or other strangers sitting nearby. When I had semi-numbed my pain, I'd get back on my bike and ride until I was sober enough to return home. These bike rides were during my first attempts to abstain from alcohol for a year.

There were periods after we had moved to Indianapolis in which I went a month or more without drinking. But time and time again, I fell back into drinking, the only way I knew to deal with pain. I gave up all of the momentum I had created for a few drinks at the bar. The thing about momentum is that it's not only a physical force; it's a psychological and emotional one as well. I knew what I was doing was wrong, and I beat myself up over it constantly. It was always hanging over my head, much like the continual lies I told my family in the past.

I thought these bike rides were me being weak, falling victim to old routines, and being what society often deems a "lost cause," destined to be a drain on the system. I thought that I lacked the ability to deal with my emotions, that drinking was the only way I knew to handle difficult thoughts, feelings, and challenging periods of life. I had no family or friends in this new area, no one I felt I could turn to for advice or for the wisdom to talk me off the ledge. More concerning was the fact that my future wife and I felt more distant than the strangers I was sitting down at the bar with.

Yet, as I discovered the six human needs—something we'll cover in-depth next chapter—and began to write about them and their impact on my choices during this period, it became so obvious. These trips weren't only about a way to deal with or suppress my emotions. They were about a desperate attempt to meet my needs. They were attempts to, if only through casual bar talk, find connection at a point in my life when I had none. It was a way to find certainty, because as a newly engaged man dealing with new challenges, I needed a way to be certain that things would work out.

While writing this book, I came across an article that studied the innate human need for connection. The author said, "If we can't connect with each other, we will connect with anything we can find . . . "

I must have reread that at least five or six times. *Of course we will,* I thought. Sure, I had connections with other people, but as those relationships began to be tested by my actions, it was alcohol that was always there when I needed it. It sounds pathetic, I get it. Unfortunately, it's true. That need for connection is within all of us, but for some it drives us to do things we would never otherwise think of doing. It's a need we can't deny, and failing to find it with other people will only ever result in succeeding to find it wherever we can.

I knew Brittany wouldn't have wanted me to go to the bar. That's exactly why I kept it a secret and biked until I was sober afterward. Addiction, like life itself, is a complicated, deep, and difficult thing to navigate. We always have and probably always will continue to underestimate its true power. It's only through personal experience, or a great degree of empathy, that we can begin to truly understand it.

While I will admit life isn't long enough, even if we're fortunate enough to make it into our eighties or nineties, I do believe that we have to truly appreciate how long it is. It's important to have that perspective, because it helps us realize that these minor steps down the wrong path aren't going to destroy us. We need to understand that our long-term commitment will overcome any short-term, desperate reach to satisfy our needs. That long-term commitment will almost always overcome any desire to revert back to our past.

TO BUILD A SOLID STRUCTURE, YOU'LL NEED A SOLID SUPPORT SYSTEM

I spent the last few years of my teens and the first few years of my twenties trying to undo whatever I did the night—or, often, the month—before. It was a constant battle between the person I was when under the influence and the person I was when thinking clearly. Aside from the occasional clouded judgment while riding my bike to the bar, I was on a mostly straight and narrow path. Over four hundred miles separated me from my small hometown in central Wisconsin and all the bad influences that resided there.

Britt and I worked through many of the challenges that led us to postpone our wedding initially. We had rescheduled it a few months later, for November, which was fast approaching. We scheduled our wedding shower a few months prior and took a trip home to celebrate with our friends and family.

Our shower was at a local bar/small reception facility in our hometown. As you can expect, it was easy to revert back to the past life I had fought hard to leave when surrounded by familiar faces and locations. It was like muscle memory, a switch being flipped that caused me to lose control of my mind, body, and actions. I drank moderately during the day. We socialized, ate, and opened gifts. But sometime between Britt leaving to go hang out with her friends and returning to pick me up a few hours later, I became belligerently drunk.

Laughter and music filled the open bar area. I picked up the heavy glass mug and tipped it up to allow the last swallow to drain from it. I was setting it down as the entrance door opened to reveal my Brittany and two of her friends.

"Shit . . ." I said to myself, hoping that she was just stopping in to say hi. I had already made plans to go over to a friend's house for a gathering of continued drinking and getting high. The closing of the door behind Brittany and her friends symbolized the likely closing of my desires for the night to continue. Clearly she would be able to tell that I was too drunk already.

"Ready to go?" Britt asked as she came over by me.

"I don't know. What are your plans for the rest of the night?" I replied.

"Me and the girls are going to go hang out over at my parents' house for the rest of the night. You should invite some friends over."

"That's okay, I'm going to go over by Haley's house to hang out with some friends there. Why don't you and your girlfriends just hang out, since you don't get to see them that often?" I replied, trying not to sound suspicious.

"Jake, you've had enough to drink. You don't need to continue drinking. Have them come over to my parents' and we can hang there."

"All right, let's go," I said as I stood up and wandered over to the door and out to the vehicle. Britt and I got into one car while her friends got into their car to follow us. When she got in I reiterated my plans. "I'm going to my friend's house."

"Jake, no you're not. You're beyond drunk. You're going home to pass out," Britt said matter-of-factly.

"It's early yet. I'm not going to bed. You better drop me off at my friend's house. I'm not going to your parents'!"

"I don't care what you say. You're not going over to your friend's to get high. You know I don't like it, and you've already had way too much to drink."

I was caught off guard as I realized she was aware of my plans. Apparently I'd left my phone out when going to the bathroom, and she saw the conversation between my friends and me. "Quit being such a bitch and take me to my friend's house!" I yelled and cursed at her to try and get my way.

"No," she said, calmly but firmly.

I was only getting angrier that my night wasn't ending how I wanted it to. As we were driving down the main street in our town, I reached over, turned the car off, and pulled the key out of the ignition. "I'm not going to your parents."

"What the hell, Jake?! You're going to get us into an accident." Britt said as she coasted to the side of the road to attempt to grab the key from me so that we could continue driving.

"I'm not going to your fucking parents' house!" I yelled, throwing the key into the cup holder.

Britt grabbed it, turned the car back on, and continued driving. "Yes you are. You're not drinking any more."

I continued yelling and cursing at her while we drove a few more miles. Adamant that I was not ready to call it a night, I pulled the key out of the ignition again, and when we had slowed down enough, I got out of the car and began walking through parking lot we had coasted into. Britt's friends pulled in slowly behind us, surely curious of what had been going on as they followed behind us.

"Jake, get back here!" Britt said firmly as I got out of the car. We argued in a parking lot for a few more minutes while her friends looked from their vehicle and I made a complete ass out of myself. Britt called my dad out of desperation to try to figure out what to do. As my dad was talking to her, my last drinks caught up with me, and I blacked out. I suppose blacking out was to everyone's benefit, because I finally gave in and rode back to Britt's parents' house to pass out alone on the couch.

I woke up the next morning, as one often does after a serious event, feeling the weight of my actions. I couldn't recall everything, but I could sense that I had messed up. Also, Britt's dad helped me fill in some details as he talked to me shortly after waking up.

"Jake, you're an angry and mean drunk. Some people can drink, manage it, and have fun—but you, you're an angry drunk," he said.

As I mentioned in the beginning of the book, it can be fun to sit around with friends and piece back together the previous night's escapade. Not so fun is sitting down with your future father-in-law and looking him in the eyes while he tells you the things you did and said to his daughter, your future wife. Today, I write this as a father to my own two beautiful boys; it remains a mystery to me how he didn't Hulk-smash my ignorant, immature ass until I had some sense knocked into me or the stupidity knocked out of me.

Those words hit me hard. Not only was I mean and angry, but I'd done that to my future wife, the woman who helped me straighten my path in the first place. It was hard to swallow, but I couldn't deny it. I agreed with everything he had said.

"Brittany isn't sure she wants to marry you anymore after how you treated her last night."

I couldn't believe I'd damaged so much of what was good in my life in such a short period of time. Not only that, I was now sober and could clearly see the work I'd have to do to repair it. My drunken tantrum didn't force Britt to call off our pending wedding, but it did leave a lot of work for me to prove that I was still someone she wanted to marry. To be honest, if it wasn't for us expecting our first child in seven or eight months, it's likely she would've called it off, and I wouldn't have blamed her one bit.

This one night was a wrecking ball to the guts that knocked me back a good hundred yards, undoing months and months of solid steps forward. I was now trying to evolve into someone who didn't need to rely on alcohol, who could be an amazing husband and father and live the life he wanted to live. This two-hour period from that one night luckily turned out to be only a setback, not a complete descent to rock bottom. That has little to do with me and everything to do with my wife, the amazing woman who stuck by my side and trusted that I could overcome my struggles with alcohol. From that point on, I realized just how committed I needed to be to the marathon of trying to turn my life around.

Overcoming adversity, accomplishing dreams, conquering addiction, being a great spouse/father/son/daughter/friend/person, or creating something profound has to be looked at as a marathon. If you try to sprint your way through hard times, you'll get burnt out and give up, ending not far from where you tried to start. However, if you look at it as a marathon and yourself as an amateur runner (because no one is a professional in the game of life), it becomes a journey that is much more manageable. In a marathon, passing one person is a small victory. Sure, you can have a little celebration, even give yourself a pat on the back, but you don't stop just because you accomplished one small goal. A marathon requires much more than small bursts of all-out effort. Whether you intended or not, you've been training yourself for a marathon through your actions over the past months or years, and it's only a marathon of effort that can get you out.

With that commitment, I worked diligently to prove to Britt that she could trust me and I could manage my drinking. If anything, that drunken tantrum showed me that I couldn't only rely on my desire to change. Clearly, when the right ingredients came together, no matter my drive and determination for a better future, I was almost powerless and reverted back a much more obnoxious, pitiful Jake.

We drove back to Indianapolis the day after our wedding shower. It was a quiet, eight-hour drive back home. It was sometime over those next few weeks, while listening to a podcast at work, that I had heard a quote that changed everything for me:

It seems like such common sense, but it forced me to fully grasp the very real truth; if I was going to make it past these occasional pulls to a life I fought hard to leave, I would need people who supported me along that journey. Drinking—something most people, including my friends back home, could do moderately and in a controlled manner— was undoubtedly not possible for me. I needed to surround myself with people who challenged me to grow as a person, who encouraged me to do better, and who didn't have alcohol or drugs as a prerequisite to spending time together.

We were nearing the end of 2014, shortly after Brittany and I got married. I had left the house and gone for a drive after Britt and I had gotten into a fight. I was so sick of being depressed, feeling empty, not knowing how to get back the amazing relationship I once had with the girl I loved, and wanting to solve it all with alcohol. I pulled into a Starbucks parking lot, did a Google search, and made a call to schedule an appointment with a counselor to help me straighten my life out and work through some questions I had.

I sat down for several sessions to work through my own issues, and then Brittany eventually joined in so that we could work through our challenges as newlyweds. I needed to learn how to treat her better if we were ever going to last. I needed to learn how to control or stop my drinking if I was ever going to pursue the life I wanted to live. It was through those counseling sessions that I realized how important a tool good communication is.

I'm one of those people who holds everything in, letting the pressure build up until I'm annoyed and pissed off and can't possibly "just deal with it" one more day. So I blow up and unload a month's worth of issues all at once, and then I get over it until next time. If you're one of those people, you've probably realized how ineffective it is, especially in marriage.

I came to understand that communicating thoroughly with my wife would help clear up confusion before it had the chance to arise. Communication allowed me to gain control of my travels back home by telling my friends that I was only available to meet up for coffee, instead of the previous norm—going out for drinks. It's funny how quickly my list of friends shrunk from dozens to the two or three who were willing to join me for coffee. When I had control, I could begin implementing the greatest life hack of all—changing who I spent my time with.

My counselor brought me a greater understanding of myself. Podcasts, books, and other forms of personal development brought about a greater sense of control over my life. I began surrounding myself, both physically and virtually, with everyone from whom I could pull wisdom and positive vibes, and who gave me the best chance of making the right choices.

Speaking of podcasts, I happened to listen to an interview while going through the final edits of the book that I couldn't help but add in. Mark Zuckerberg, the founder of Facebook, was being interviewed by Stephen Dubner, the host of the Freakonomics podcast. Zuckerberg said that while speaking to a group of former and recovering heroin addicts, every single one admitted that they relapsed 100 percent of the time when continuing to be friends with the same crowd who got them there in the first place. The only way they were able to escape was to cut out the relationships that kept dragging them back to a life they were trying to leave.

We're living through, in my well-rounded opinion and despite what your news channel will tell you, one of the most incredible times in history. You can literally pick up your phone right now and tune into the podcast or YouTube channel or Facebook page of someone who inspires you, educates you, and encourages you to live the life you want, a life that matters far beyond a few hours in the bar on a Saturday night. You can send an email, tweet, or direct message to that person and often get a response. You can see who *they* follow to learn from and be inspired by. Do more of that, and I promise that your life will look completely different.

Every day, I did my best to make the right choices and pass just one more person on the marathon I was running—that we're all running. Those bike rides to the bar were eventually replaced with a much-improved relationship with my wife. My drinking and getting high to suppress the painful work of dealing with uncomfortable thoughts and feelings was replaced with counseling, more open communication, and a new circle of friends. Through all of this, it became much easier to trust the process of going from where I was to where I wanted to be. Not every day was a victory, but it was a necessary step in my journey to become the person who currently writes this book.

If you're ever going to stand on solid ground, laying the bricks of your unique structure with the foundation of rock bottom beneath you, it is crucial that you commit to this process and allow yourself to make mistakes. I promise you that you'll slip up. I guarantee that people will try to drag you back down and keep you from leaving them behind. I assure you that your past will try to influence and trick you, promising a taste of the sweetness you miss without any of the bitterness that motivated you to leave it behind in the first place. However, not a single one of those things will come close to the feeling of pride obtained from overcoming a dark past filled with adversity or living a life closer to the one you desire.

Whatever you have gone through, whatever you are going through, whatever you will go through, however big or small it seems, the life you want and deserve to live is worth every ounce of energy you have to give. Do it for yourself, and from that you will be able to work toward everything else you've always wanted. For now, just focus on your next step. Remain patient until it becomes unbearably annoying, and then continue to remain patient. I promise you, it's not only necessary; it's worth it.

"Knowing yourself
is the beginning
of all wisdom."

———

Aristotle

9

KNOW YOURSELF BEFORE YOU CAN CHANGE YOURSELF

I suppose it seems odd that I put a chapter about knowing yourself before you can change yourself near the end of the book, but I promise it'll make sense. It wasn't all that long ago that I began the journey of trying to know myself and to better understand what I wanted from life. I was in the early stages of writing this book, and my wife, my two kids, and I were living just outside of Washington, DC. We had been there about six months and were anxious to leave once I finished my yearlong commitment for my job.

Every morning I woke up, got ready, made coffee, wrote for an hour, and drove to work. It wasn't far to my office, but with DC traffic, an otherwise ten-minute drive often took thirty minutes or more. The commute never bothered me, though, because I'm a podcast addict, and I always had plenty of episodes to catch up on. I love when I'm listening to a podcast and someone's story, a bit of advice, or an all-out knowledge bomb is dropped on me—giving me goose bumps, making me rethink a belief I hold, or opening my eyes to a certain topic.

It was no surprise to me that while listening to Tony Robbins's podcast I was drawn in for the entirety of my thirty-minute commute. One moment I had goose bumps. The next moment I had to pause the episode to process the thoughts in my head. In roughly thirty minutes I had come to understand more about my life than I had ever before—specifically, why I do the things I do. If there is one event in my life that has been close to an epiphany, it was that entire thirty-minute commute to work while listening to the episode of the Tony Robbins Podcast "Why We Do What We Do."

First, let me give a quick bio of who Tony is, as you may not be familiar with him. He's mostly known for being an entrepreneur, motivational speaker, author, and philanthropist, but he's much more than that. I could go on and on about who he is and rattle off many more titles, but just know that he's widely seen as a top leadership and self-development expert. He has also advised a person or two you may have heard of, from Serena Williams to numerous presidents to Wayne Gretzky to multibillionaires. In short, he's someone worth following and knowing about.

This episode I listened to made clear some of the biggest missing pieces of my entire life and addressed some of its biggest question marks. Why did I have to hit rock bottom before making a change? What was it about alcohol that made me so susceptible to its grip? What could I do to ensure I never fell back into my previous lifestyle?

The title, "Why We Do What We Do," is based around the fact that the motivation behind our actions is fueled primarily by six things: our core human needs. Robbins says: "These needs are not merely wants or desires, but profound needs and the basis of every choice we make."

The first four needs are needs of the personality:

1. Certainty: the need to avoid pain, be in control, and plan ahead
2. Uncertainty (variety): the need for excitement, spontaneity, and living in the moment
3. Significance: the need to feel unique, special, and important
4. Love (connection): the need to love, be loved, and have great relationships

The remaining two needs are the needs of the spirit. Unlike the first four, which everyone will find a way to meet, not everyone will meet these last two.

5. Growth: the need for progress and being a part of something bigger

6. Contribution: the need to give back and share our overflowing life and emotions with others

I will go into detail about this topic, but I can't possibly cover everything, as the psychology behind it and implementation of it could be entire books by themselves. Much like the rest of the ideas I've covered so far, if you want to see results, you're going to have to work at it daily.

Everyone will find a way—whether short term or long term, constructively or destructively—to meet the first four human needs. The difference between us is the amount of value we associate with each one. For example, certainty and significance are most important to me, but I also need to have a level of love and uncertainty in my life. Growth and contribution are necessary whenever we have an abundance of life to live and give. There's a balance between each of these six needs. That, once again, is the hard part. It's up to us to do the digging required to determine which ones we value most and then find ways in which we can meet our needs constructively thereafter.

Equipped with this introductory understanding, I want you to follow my story while also looking very honestly and openly at your life. You may have realized the recurrence of this theme; you've already gone through most of this book, and with it, I hope you've done a fair amount of reflecting on the years you've lived. Through that reflection, you've already begun your journey into living a life that matters. I only want you to continue along it, tearing apart the framework and looking to see what may be hiding that will force you to look at your life and others' from a different perspective. By reading and applying the content within this chapter, you will be able to better implement everything learned in a way that will best suit you and your unique needs.

The previous chapters have helped lay the groundwork for you to dig yourself out of rock bottom or avoid it altogether. I want to give you the tools to avoid it for good. This chapter, albeit near the end of the book, was put here for a reason. It's probably the single most important chapter in this book, but without the earlier chapters, it won't help you in the slightest. If you can successfully implement the content earlier in this book, then this chapter will change your life forever. Naturally, we must gain a level of understanding about ourselves, as the earlier chapters aim to do, before we can effectively change ourselves.

A KEY TO THE PAST AND A SOLID FOUNDATION FOR YOUR FUTURE

It wasn't until the last few years that I began choosing and creating my own life—that is, making conscious decisions instead of allowing life to happen to me. Until that point, I was mostly reacting to my environment and subconsciously fulfilling my needs the easiest way possible. It's fascinating to me how we instinctively meet our human needs, whether we intend to or not. Human needs are at the core of human life, and they drive everything we do. They control every decision we make.

What makes it most difficult is that our brain is an efficient machine that will do all it can to conserve energy. Our brain wants to satisfy our needs as easily as possible, and easy means immediate rewards that usually come with long-term consequences. To get the endorphins that follow an accomplishment, the creation of something, or doing anything worthwhile is to fight the friction required to take it from start to finish. Alternatively, we can choose to walk the resistance-free downhill path to endorphins by sucking down a case of beer, pulling the slot-machine handle, or smoking a cigarette. Both the hard and easy option will make you feel good, but in different ways. One is the working of a successful life, and the other, if not done in moderation, is a guaranteed dead end.

I chose the easy path for many years. It wasn't until that day on my couch that I knew my life would only turn around once I began choosing a different—and, likely, more challenging—path. That morning in my car, when I learned of the human needs and how I could use them to understand my past and guide my future, I felt empowered to finally create and live the life I had always wanted. It felt as though all of the work I had committed to over the three or four years prior to that moment was finally coming together.

ROUTINES: THE GOOD, THE BAD, AND THE UGLY

Robbins's voice filled my car, and goose bumps covered my arms. I pulled into the parking spot at my work and sat in my car to finish the remaining five or ten minutes of the episode. I grabbed my phone to take a few notes. One thing that kept running through my mind was something Tony said near the beginning of the episode: "Once you understand these six human needs, you'll no longer see the people's crazy behavior; you'll see their desperate attempts to meet their needs."

Images of me dancing on tables in bars, passing out in booths, and shouting obscenities at random strangers flashed through my mind.

Our needs are constant. The ways in which we meet them don't have to be.

You can get certainty through smoking a cigarette, and you can get it through working out intensely. You can get certainty by getting really angry and pissed off to ensure you get your way. You can get certainty by being under the influence of drugs or alcohol. You can find significance in being a good, influential person, or you can find it by being a terrible bully. When we continually meet our needs via a regular activity or tactic, it likely has become embedded into our lives, rather than serving as something we do on occasion. A routine, one might say.

A routine, whether good or bad, is a powerful tool that humans utilize often. Routines help to condense time and bring about a sense of monotony that we follow from A to B to C. Successful people arrange and utilize routines as a productivity hack in order to batch the day's most important tasks together without interruption. On the opposite end of the spectrum are the people who most often fall into the routines that only serve to hinder their growth by way of those seemingly small, harmless decisions you read about earlier. They form a bad habit or two and then turn them into daily rituals that only do harm. I'm sure that, as you read this, you can easily identify your daily activities that are doing you harm.

Drinking was my way of gaining certainty at a time when I otherwise had none. I could replace any amount of fear and anxiety for the future with alcohol, and that was all the certainty I needed. Drinking afforded me connection with others, whether it was my friends or strangers at the bar. I was often able to gain significance, which came in the form of buying drinks for others, being the designated (drunk) driver, or simply hedging all of my bets on being so obnoxiously drunk that no one could ignore me.

Right now it may seem easy to understand how routines, whether good or bad, form and why they can be so hard to break. Our human needs are the foundation for why we do what we do, and if what we're doing is meeting our needs—especially if we're doing so with little effort—it takes an incredible amount of effort in the opposite direction to break free from that routine.

So, then, where does our hope lie? It lies in our desire for a future. One that doesn't leave us waking up feeling insignificant and beaten up by a life that never amounted to anything. Meeting our needs in a destructive manner is effective, but it's not efficient, at least not long term. Meeting our needs constructively is both effective and efficient, and it offers us long-term rewards.

Let me put this in context for you: a handful of months into writing this book, I had a deep, long talk with a good friend. It had been a bit since we spoke, so we caught up a bit and then dug into the deeper parts of conversation that I love to explore. He slowly began opening up about what he was experiencing and why life was a bit challenging at the moment.

He'd had an innate passion for baseball since he could throw a ball. His time playing had mostly come to an end, so naturally, he had begun umping behind home plate. It was his calling, his passion, his purpose—call it what you want. From the outside looking in, his dreams of becoming a major-league umpire seemed all but certain to come true. People who have that kind of fire and drive for the things they want always seem to get them because, often, that's how life works; you put in the work, do a good job, remain persistent, and get rewarded.

Shortly after he had completed some education and training at a major-league umpire school, my friend began traveling around the US to umpire minor-league baseball games. The dream was in his grasp, and all he was missing was persistence. Unfortunately, every now and then, life grabs the biggest wrench it has and hurls it into the hopes, dreams, and plans we had, wiping out every possibility of pursuing them any further. My friend sustained his third severe concussion while umping and was told that he would not be able to continue. He ran the risk of it happening again, causing serious, irreversible damage, and the league wouldn't allow it.

Here my friend was, with years of time and work devoted to a lifelong passion, now having to rethink everything he had dreamt about becoming since he was a little kid. Something that many umpires can go an entire career without encountering, a concussion, was preventing him from pursuing it any further. I had learned of the six human needs shortly before this conversation, so it was easy for me to appreciate why baseball meant so much to him. It was basically a constructive addiction. It provided him certainty by way of his making calls and having a level of control over the game. It provided uncertainty through the variety of games, players, and locations. You don't need to know much about baseball to know that a home-plate umpire is a significant part of the game. He received connection from other players and the regular umpiring crew he usually traveled with. He also received growth and contribution simply by doing his job, getting better at it, and volunteering to ump kids' games while back home.

This new reality wasn't one he had planned for. Upon returning home, he began going to the little hole-in-the-wall neighborhood bar close to his house for food and the occasional drink. Without realizing it, he started replacing baseball with alcohol to fulfill his needs.

"Do you feel like you're drinking more than you want to?" I asked him.

"I mean, I don't think I'm an alcoholic by any means, but I definitely feel like I drink too much, and I want to drink less," he said in a tone that lacked the confidence he once overflowed with. "I want to be doing something else, but I'm having trouble figuring it out."

"Man, do I know how you feel there," I said, hoping to comfort him by letting him know he wasn't alone.

Just three short years earlier, I was looking at his life thinking, *Man, he has it all figured out.* He was getting to travel and was being paid rather well to do so, not to mention pursuing his lifelong dreams. Fast-forward to our conversation, and he thought I currently had it all together while he saw his past five or six years of hard work slowly unraveling into nightly drinks at a local dive bar after working a part-time job he had little excitement for.

I was three years removed from a routine that hurled me to rock bottom. Listening to my friend's story, I could see that he was slowly constructing the same routine I had fought so hard to leave. He knew my story, and with the lessons and experiences I shared with him, knew that his choices were slowly leading him to a very similar destination. It should be relatively easy to understand why the life he was reluctantly living would remain unchanged unless he knew why he was doing what he was doing and had the deep desire to change his life.

I could have sent him every podcast, website, and article that so much as referenced the six human needs, but unless the earlier content of this book was in practice, the desire to change existed, and a bit of luck appeared, his life was going to continue along its relatively predictable trajectory. Ultimately, there is not one thing that I've ever come across or know to exist that will fix our lives for us entirely; that task falls almost fully on our individual shoulders.

I'm convinced while writing this that some people will never overcome their adversity. We see it daily through homeless people living on the streets, the massive drug problems destroying communities and lives across the US, health-related matters out of control, consumer debt rising consistently through the roof, and job satisfaction ratings stagnating at roughly 20 percent. Maybe the biggest problem of all is that we only ever treat the symptoms instead of looking closely at the root cause.

No one wakes up one day and decides they want to take the treacherous, long, and winding road to the depths of rock bottom. Yes, as I've talked about previously, it's our choices that lead us there; that's the why. "Why did you reach rock bottom?" Simply put, because I made bad choices. However, there's so much more to it than the why, because the why is fueled by the what. "What led you to make those choices?" There is no way to simply or quickly express that answer. If someone ever does bring that question up, you might want to tell them to grab some coffee and take a seat. Drug addicts don't become addicted because they think it would make their family proud. Homeless people don't become homeless because they like taking your pocket change from you. Obese people don't become obese because they like getting judged while buying a pint of ice cream. I'm not going to attempt to discern the infinite reasons why people reach the countless varieties of addiction and paths to rock bottom, but I do know what leads them there.

> *"People will give up on their hopes and dreams to meet their needs."*
>
> —Tony Robbins

ADDICTION IS ALLOWING YOUR NEEDS TO BE MET IN A DESTRUCTIVE WAY

In her book *Hunger*, Roxane Gay shares, "When I was twelve years old I was raped and then I ate and ate and ate to build my body into a fortress."

At the risk of coming off as though I'm trying to sum up her life's work in one short quote, I'd like to say that life isn't, for any one of us, simple, concrete, or objective. I think she'd agree with that.

After seeing some examples of human needs and how we tend to meet them, it may seem obvious to you why Roxane Gay may have, as she puts it, built her body into a fortress. Doing so was a way of gaining certainty, avoiding pain, and taking back control when a nasty human being took that, and so much more, away from her. Food became that control, and much like alcohol did for me, it also became a place of comfort and connection.

My questions surrounding the why became much clearer while listening to Robbins's podcast than they were at any other time. "How many of you have something on your list where you're doing dumbass things to meet some of your needs, and even though it doesn't meet all of your needs, it meets some of them, and so you keep on doing them?" Robbins asked his live audience on the podcast. I thought about it most of the day, and by the time I was ready to go home, I had several sticky notes filled with notes and questions to examine later.

I came home from work that afternoon with this information and tried to figure out how I could implement it into this book. After spending time with our kids and laying them down for bed, my wife and I went up to the loft in our apartment to work. I was skimming over all of the notes I had written throughout the day, and the first thing that came to mind was that summer camping trip with my family, when I got drunk for the first time. That was really the first point in my life when my needs (which I was unaware of at the time), were satisfied so effectively.

It was still mostly an innocent night, but the fact that it met my innate needs for connection and attention so easily allowed it to become more than only a one-off event. It made other events in the future easier to say yes to, because I had already broken down the barrier.

Most of us have stories like my night around the campfire. Not necessarily stories about getting wasted when we were fourteen but, rather, moments that were pivotal in our lives which we've never taken the time to process. For you it may be a difficult breakup, a fight between your parents, or someone telling you, "You'll never amount to anything," or, "You're going to do great things." Whatever it is, exploring those events will help make sense not only of the events themselves but also of every event that spun off from them and led you to where you are today.

If there's one thing I feel it's necessary to mention at this point, it's that although our choices are ultimately and exactly that—our choices—we can't deny the fact that there is a portion of our lives that we can't control. We like to believe the stories of someone who "made it"—that it was entirely because of their hard work, brilliant decision making, and perseverance. And, when someone spends years of their life drudging through misery and maybe even contemplating suicide, we also tend to believe it was all their doing—if only they'd had a little more self-control or not been so dumb, they wouldn't be where they are.

In any given day, there are an unimaginable number of variables that can force us to change our plans, derail our mood, and make life difficult. Heavy traffic delays our commute, we spill coffee on our clothes, our kids are crabby, we miss an appointment by a few minutes, we have to stay late at work, or our supervisor Dave is being a miserable person—the variables go on and on. It's easy to see how the falling apart of any random day occurs, but we neglect to see the big picture of someone attaining great success or diving deep into adversity for what it really is: a million micro-events that came together over time to construct that success or adversity.

I've seen and heard firsthand that much of our adversity begins like mine—with hopes and dreams but no real plan on how to get there. The problems worsen when we aren't aware of our needs and we meet them with the assistance of those countless variables that exist within all of our lives: family and friends who are bad influences, a string of bad luck that tightens our finances, or emotional challenges. All of these things are mostly out of our control, yet they play a significant role in determining the overall trajectory of our individual days, which come together to form our life. These influences trickle in and nudge us ever so slightly off of our path. Then, by our own choosing, we go with it, which only helps reinforce the effectiveness of that choice in meeting our needs.

It's through the stringing together of those individual days that the ways in which we're meeting our needs become vital. You read about the long-term effect of those small steps down the wrong path a few chapters back, so I'm not going to continue beating on it. But it's imperative that we regularly take time to assess the choices we're making and whether or not they're meeting our needs constructively.

I'm not so sure there is anything we humans won't do to meet our needs. We'll tell ourselves and others lies; we'll disregard our values; we'll give up on our dreams; we'll trade away our health; and we'll destroy friendships, all in the name of satisfying our needs.

This is why knowing who we are and what our needs are is so important. Once we understand what our needs are, we're able to make clear decisions as to how we can best satisfy them in a constructive manner. If we aren't aware of our needs, we'll still meet them, but we'll gravitate toward the easiest methods, rather than by means that empower us. We tend to prefer the quick fix (the sugar high), rather than the long-term hard work and skill of being 100 percent honest with ourselves in this entire process of choosing and living a life that matters.

HOW DOES ADVERSITY BECOME A THING OF THE PAST?

My family and I had made it home for the holidays. A few days into our time there, I sat down for some coffee with Eric, a man I consider to be my mentor, a best friend, and a model for what it means to be a phenomenal human being always striving for more. It was actually the first time we had ever met in person. Our wives had introduced us a few years prior—we really clicked and had continued talking every few months or so since then. He's a fellow veteran and someone whose story shares many common threads with mine.

"Have you ever heard of the six human needs?" I asked him after he had mentioned his search for certainty through his actions.

"I have," he replied. "I've actually studied them heavily and am going through a program that covers them more in depth right now."

I wasn't surprised. Eric is always psychoanalyzing himself and is able to provide clear insight as to why he thought, felt, and did specific things in his life.

He went on: "It's why I drank massive amounts of alcohol and consumed excessive quantities of drugs. They gave me a sense of certainty, because without them I knew very well the horror that accompanied me as I attempted to fall asleep. With alcohol, cocaine, and late nights partying, I could go until I physically couldn't go anymore and then pass out easily. It's easy to find connection and certainty in the traditional babes, beards, bullets, and booze, which men—more specifically, men after returning home from a deployment—often resort to."

I chuckled at this truth and at the recollections of conversations I'd had with men who wholly believed that these were what defined a man. We're not supposed to be vulnerable and talk about feelings, but that's exactly what needs to be done if we're going to satisfy our needs constructively and sustainably.

Seeing the effects of the six human needs on Eric, someone who had been aware of and living them out in his own life for some time, was reassuring. I knew of their effectiveness through my own experience, but it felt good knowing that a concept I cover at length in this chapter was incredibly valuable to someone whom I deeply respect and admire for his wisdom. His story is just one of the countless I have heard that inspire me to be more and do more. It's why I know that you and your unique story are also worthy of being more and doing more, no matter how much hell you might currently be going through or how much self-confidence you lack.

With the knowledge of why you do the things you do, you can

begin choosing things that are constructive. Honestly, the most difficult part of the choice between the constructive and the destructive isn't knowing what you should or shouldn't be doing; most of us know what we should be doing most of the time. We don't need someone to tell us that we shouldn't pass out in the corner booth of bars, put a needle filled with drugs in our arm, chase money simply for the sake making ourselves feel better, or perform any other activity that allows us to mask the pain we feel and delay dealing with it until a later time. The hard part is running toward our fear, the unknown, the uncomfortable, the pain, and the suppressed thoughts and feelings, and then doing the things that don't always feel good instantly but will reward us for the rest of our lives.

We can't ignore our pain, and we can't run from our past or the choices we've made and the wreckage we've left behind us. Instead, we must work to uncover the ways in which we can meet our needs in a constructive, sustainable manner.

Pain and adversity are inevitable. They're a byproduct of life. We're all going to experience them at some point, for some amount of time, for some undesired reason. No matter what form the pain comes in, it inevitably lies along our path, no matter how perfectly we plan our life. It's in those moments when pain attempts to derail us that we must focus extra intently on our dreams, our goals, our needs, and the ways in which we meet them that allow us to keep moving forward constructively.

Addictions can be broken, pain can be diminished, and problems can be defeated. However, if we fail to understand why any of it entered our lives in the first place, it will refuse to go away and only continue to cycle through, until it eventually kills us or we naturally reach the end of our lives never having understood why they seemed to be missing something. We must understand on an intimate level why we chose to start smoking cigarettes, drinking excessively, stealing from our employer, giving up on our dreams, cheating on our spouse, or getting into fights. Whatever the addiction, pain, or problem is, no matter how much it hurts, it can be dealt with in a productive manner.

As you read in the chapter on lifelines, I hope this book can be something you cling to and that can help pull you from the undesirable path you're on. Life provides us plenty of opportunities to escape from the path we're on, but just like the lifeline, we need to spot them when they appear. It's in these moments of grabbing the lifeline that we are most open to changing the trajectory of our life.

My trajectory prior to going on that second deployment is something I find myself thinking about often—mostly because I'm curious as to the alternate paths my life could've gone down had I not spent that last twenty, made the decision to reroute my life, and put myself in position to say yes to that deployment. I'd probably be homeless or working a minimum-wage job, overall despising the life I never intended to live.

It was only because I was doing some of the right things that I had the opportunity to date Brittany and eventually make her my wife. Throughout that journey to improve my life, I gained confidence in who I could be and went from knowing what I should be doing to following through on actually doing it.

Possibly, much like me, you'll go about your life like I did for years, thinking you're invincible and that "it'll never happen to you." All I ask is one thing: when either you prove me wrong (you were invincible) or I prove you wrong (you weren't invincible), send me an email to let me know.

However, I certainly hope that isn't the case. I hope you decide today that your future will stop looking like your past and that the life you've always dreamt of will no longer be a dream but will instead be a pursuit and, perhaps, a future.

THE JOURNEY EVOLVES, BUT IT NEVER ENDS

From the years of 2009 through 2013, I lived a life that consisted largely of the overconsumption of, and eventual addiction to, alcohol and drugs. The funny thing is that I never saw my drinking as an issue, just like a fish doesn't know it's in water. My behavior while drunk was accepted, viewed as entertaining, and even celebrated—and, because of my surroundings, it was not viewed as an issue. Also worth mentioning is the insane behavior one has to perform and the quantities of alcohol one has to drink to be classified as an alcoholic in our society. I hear it all the time: "Well, he just has a little drinking thing," "She definitely likes to drink," "That's just who he is." We justify insanity simply because alcohol was a factor.

From 2014 to the present, I have lived a life that consisted largely of unlearning everything I devoted much of my time to since I was a teen. I learned that it's almost become taboo to talk negatively about alcohol and that even undeniable alcoholics aren't viewed as people in need of help. There are alcoholics, and then every other subset of addict you could possibly be. "They've always been a drinker," we say, as if to diminish our responsibility to them or to somehow justify their choices as something other than the issue they are. We place alcohol on this pedestal, separate from other drugs, substances, activities, and overall addictions.

People addicted to gambling are degenerates and fools. People addicted to cell phones are lazy and worthless. People addicted to food are disgusting. People addicted to sex are liars and pigs. People addicted to drugs are deadbeats and scum. People addicted to cigarettes are weak and gross.

People addicted to alcohol are our Uncle Joey, Cousin Beth, good friend Jordan, and Grandpa Frank. We often justify or deny the amount of alcohol they drink so as to not classify them as alcoholics at all, or we say "fun" thinks like, "They've always been a drinker," "Oh, Tanya just loves her wine," or "That's just a part of who Derek is."

Even if we do acknowledge someone's addiction, in general, we don't come close to understanding the death grip it so often has on their entire life. When I tried to stop drinking for a year, I used to walk down the beer and liquor aisles in the grocery store just to see the shelves filled with some of my favorite beers, wishing I could open them and take a strong, lengthy sniff of the hoppy, carbonated scent being released from the mouth of the bottle. After a few minutes had passed and I had talked myself out of putting any alcohol in my cart, I would go on to finish the rest of my grocery shopping.

Other times, I would drop a make-your-own-six-pack into my cart, but by the time I finished my grocery shopping I would have talked myself out of buying it and placed it on a random aisle end cap before reaching the checkout. I made my own nonalcoholic bloody Marys to help curb my cravings. Yes, all of this is harmless, but it clearly shows the psychological pull addiction has.

In 2014 and 2015, I tried to go a year without drinking, but it wasn't until 2016 that I was able to successfully complete that goal. After being alcohol-free in 2016, I christened the success by enjoying one of my favorite beers, a hefeweizen. Before it was halfway gone, I could sense that familiar feeling coming over me. My face was warm and tingly. I felt relaxed, and the motivation to continue writing this book had mostly drained from me by the time I finished the bottle. I became tired and only wanted one of two things: to go to sleep or drink a few more.

I turned to Britt, who was sitting beside me in our apartment loft and asked, "Can I tell you something?"

"Sure," she said.

I paused, trying to think of the best way to say it. "If there were more in the fridge it would be hard for me not to drink them."

"Well, I don't like hearing that . . ." she replied.

"I know, but I want to be honest with you. Like, I don't think I ever could or would—because I have you and the kids and my goals and dreams to provide me motivation and drive not to fall backward—but I'm just saying that I could easily have more." I rambled on as I began to regret drinking even that one pointless beer.

I truly believe that I'm at a point now where I won't ever fall back into a life that resembles the one of years prior. But, truly, it still takes conscious effort. I still don't go out for drinks with anyone, only coffee.

After that year of abstaining from alcohol in 2016, I did have several alcoholic drinks in 2017, but simply because I was often judging myself or wanting to drink more often than I felt comfortable with I decided to take another year off from drinking again in 2018. I had some big goals I wanted to accomplish, and having my mind clouded by those thoughts wasn't going to help me be successful.

Clearly my life was not turned around overnight. It's taken me years to undo the hardwiring that I spent nearly a decade programming into my brain. The initial influence that introduced me to the path of drinking and partying was that weekend camping trip as a teenager. It might seem as though, had that event not occurred that evening, my life might have turned out much differently. That's something I've thought about on and off while writing this book. I believe it's more likely that the absence of that event would have only detoured the inevitable rather than bypassing it altogether. I believe I would've eventually discovered that alcohol was an easy way to hack my psychology and satisfy my human needs.

I was still going to find a way to meet my needs. Possibly in a better way. Possibly in a worse way. Possibly in the same way. Whatever way I fell into meeting my needs, I'm certain it wouldn't have been much different than excessive drinking. We like to tie nice, neat little bows around things so that we can clearly label the point at which our downfall began. When we do this, it simplifies things and encourages us to believe that, if only we can avoid doing that one thing, then we won't fall victim to the same perils. If only life were black and white, then that might work. As a society, we have to quit putting band-aids on wounds that are causing us to bleed out. Removing one snippet of your life will never solve the problem. It will only delay the inevitable. If I hadn't taken a drink the night of that camping trip, maybe I would have the next night, or a month later at a friend's house, or over the school year when I heard friends talking about it.

When I had finally reached rock bottom, I was left with no option but to look at myself for who I really was. That point in my life set in motion the years of work it would take to evolve past the person I was and into the person I aspired to be—someone much stronger, kinder, wiser, healthier, inspiring, and determined to help others. Evolution is a slow process. It's about tiny, unnoticeable changes over time that lead to an unrecognizably different thing.

The only thing you need to know is this: your evolution is going to happen whether you like it or not. Your daily, weekly, monthly routines are going to happen whether you consciously implement them or not. It's up to you to make a conscious decision to change for the better or to let life happen to you and, consequently, fall victim to the world around you, dealing with the leftovers of the people who chose to take control of their life.

10

AND THEN ONE DAY WE BECOME USEFUL AGAIN

It might happen when you're sitting down for dinner, walking down the street, or talking with a family member or friend that you realize how far you've come.

I can't believe it! you might think. *I did that. I refused to give up hope. I committed to myself and my future. I overcame those challenges. I learned those lessons. I fought back and reclaimed my life. I really am in control.*

At one point, our lives seemed to be a useless ball of yarn, destined for the trash. And while that's a decision many people would make due to the massive hole they need to climb out of, the lack of support they have, or any other varying reason . . . you didn't. You knew the hard work this process would require and you did it anyway. And because of that, your potential that was once disguised under a tangled mess is no longer hidden or mistaken for weakness. Because you have overcome, or are working to overcome your challenges you better understand your worth, and your potential. Now, you're untangled, free, and able to become whatever it is that you so choose.

"You must know the undeniable truth and benefit of making yourself your number one priority— and, depending on how dire your situation is, possibly your only priority. Your life deserves all you can give it."

———————

Jake Widmann

CONCLUSION

When I find myself thinking about my journey into and out of rock bottom, one primary thing comes to mind: it's easy to lose track of how much work went into both. It was while writing this book that I was able to recount, in great detail, exactly how much work both took. It might not seem like it, but it takes a fair amount of work to remain miserable and stagnant in a life you aren't satisfied with. You have to drum up a lot of excuses, justifications, and reasons for why you can't change or are destined to stay where you are. But it takes even more work to push past that life of misery and complacency into the life you dream of.

I wish I could say one specific thing was going to turn our life around; but all the money in the world, the best mentor ever, love from people who care about you, wanting a better life, reading this book, or moving to a new city—none of that will be enough. All of those things can help, but you'll also need consistency, commitment to yourself and the journey, the right choices day after day, and a profound desire to get out of and never return to your past life.

Any combination of these things, and many more—the mentors, books, people, meeting your needs constructively, desire to change—

can be the bricks of the skyscraper we're trying to build, but they're not the skyscraper itself. Each brick is as essential as the one next to it, beneath it, and above it, and only over time will you be able to step back and see the beauty that you've created.

I wish this book were an instant, foolproof fix for anyone's life. Not only would I sell a bajillion copies and become an "overnight success," but my ultimate goal, the thing I really care about—helping to end suffering and giving you the permission to live a life that matters—would be undeniably achieved.

What I can promise you is that the results you do see will be directly related to the work you put in. If you have just skimmed through this book and haven't downloaded the essential guide that accompanies it or have failed to do any of the work overcoming adversity requires, your life will remain quite the same.

If you read it and then immediately respond to your friend's text to go get drinks, cheat on your spouse, gamble, drive drunk, mindlessly scroll through Facebook for the thirteenth hour today, or make any other ill-advised choice that perpetuates the very thing you want to overcome, this book will only ever be words on pages and thoughts in the back of your mind. You need to take the action required and commit to creating your life as you desire it to be.

However, if you read this book and make just one decision to meet your needs in an empowering way, then you've created a ripple that will have a lasting impact. Let that ripple be your first step off the path you're on. Let that ripple push you a few feet closer to the lifeline you need to turn your life around. Let it lead you to a place of greater reflection, unimaginable gratitude, a desire to be more and do more, and, ultimately, the decision to never give up on creating the life you want.

If I can motivate you to do that, then I've scored a small victory. For too long, I went about my own life by seeking out the next thing that would make me feel good immediately. I don't want this book to be something that only makes you feel good and empowered when it's in your hands. I want it to be the reason you and many others have overcome adversity. I want it to be the thing you recommend to friends simply because it helped you and you believe it can help others. I want it to be the reason why you are contributing everything you were meant to contribute to the world. The best part is that, if it does even one of those things, the good feelings and empowerment will come naturally, although not always immediately.

Remember this: focus on the next small step you need to take and not on the destination. Note that I didn't say you shouldn't have a destination—rather, get clear on where you want to go and then focus on the small steps you need to take to get there, looking up occasionally to make sure you're still on track. Focusing solely on the end will surely leave you disappointed because it'll probably take longer than expected or desired.

As for you right now, in this exact moment, I want to leave you with a few pieces of actionable advice. If, after reading this book, you decide to do nothing else, or for whatever reason you simply can't bring yourself to act on any of the advice I shared, please practice these three things consistently in your life. It's these three things, in addition to what I shared in this book, that have helped to pluck me out from floating aimlessly through life and placed me on a more productive path. Not to mention, if you can do these three things, I think you'll eventually work your way toward doing everything else contained between the covers of this book.

1. Surround yourself with people who build you up, challenge you, and encourage you to be more and do more with your life.
2. Remain adamant that only you truly know what is best for your life.
3. Immerse yourself in the world around you.

SURROUND

*"Your circle of friends must match your own aspira-
tions and dreams, or you will find little support when
you need it most."*

—Leon Brown

It's no secret that we need more solid, genuine friendships with people who build us up, challenge us, and encourage us to be more and do more with our lives. It's through our relationships that our lives will either be hell, okay, or extraordinary; and you didn't pick up this book to continue walking through hell or to just be "okay." The kind of relationships I'm talking about don't allow us to wallow in our suffering. These friends are the ones who, much like my best friend Matt, will look you in the eyes, knowing what you need instead of what you want, and rather than enabling your problems will say, "What the F are you doing with your life?" or "Talk to me," or "How can I help?" Friends such as these are the ones that don't care if you have $1.50 in your bank account or $150,000.

I want to briefly clear up a common misconception about cutting ties with old friends in order to live a better life. When I began spending less time with people who I had been great friends with for years, it didn't mean that I all of a sudden thought less of them. It didn't mean that I was in any way better than them. It meant that something they could, for the most part, do responsibly (drinking), I clearly could not. It meant that they were content living the life they were living, but I was not. One is not better than the other, just different. If I was ever going to live a better life for myself, then I needed to leave drinking behind, and since they couldn't or didn't want to, I had to leave them behind as well. I still love them as the great friends they are and will never think less of them because of a weakness I struggle with.

Once you know what you want, or have a desire for something more, it's vitally important to begin surrounding yourself with people who can help you get there and to begin cutting out the people who are going to hold you back. True friends will never take offense to you putting yourself as the number-one priority in your life. If they do, they aren't true friends. One thing you can do for your own benefit is to draw a line in the sand of things you can and cannot do. Once you have that line and have made it known, your true friends will only ever help to keep you on the right side of it. One condition of my line in the sand was that I would only hang out with friends to get breakfast or coffee, not at a bar like in the past. I made it known, and the true friends that I did have gladly respected it. From there, you need to be uncompromising in sticking to your line and spending time with your friends on the right side of it or finding other ones who will.

REMAIN

"It takes courage to grow up and turn out to be who you really are."

—E. E. Cummings

This is one thing, for better or worse, I've always been able to maintain quite easily. Being annoyingly stubborn in having to figure life out on my own has caused me some of my greatest pain, but at the same time rewarded me with some of my greatest victories. It's the biggest reason I am where I am today, writing this book and actually creating something that impacts people's lives. However, it's also the biggest reason I was where I was several years ago, blacking out every time I drank and living a miserable existence.

I used to think that there was a template I needed to follow in order to find the perfect job or obtain the perfect degree—once I found it, whether that was at age twenty-four, thirty-six, or seventy-three, then I could begin living the life I actually wanted to live. That belief was why, after returning from my first deployment, I didn't want to get just a job, or go to college, or do, well, anything that was done because it was expected. Yet, as I write these words today, I also know with hindsight that using my grit to always do things my way regardless of what anyone told me was the only way I could navigate the world. However, the same may not be true for you.

My advice for you is to try to exist somewhere between the two extremes. I promise that living life the way you see fit while balanced with, at minimum, an open ear to the advice of people who care about you is a template for an ideal life. Not a life free of difficulties and challenges, because that kind of life doesn't exist, but one free of long treks down undesired paths.

One of the most valuable things you can do with your life is to never give up on that which you truly desire. Ultimately, that's what delivered me to the other side of adversity: never giving up. People will doubt you and tell you they know what's best, and you'll have to distinguish those who you can trust to offer valuable advice that can truly benefit you from those who believe there is only one recipe for success, based off the one they chose rather than the one you actually want. Those people deserve zero seconds of your time.

It's a fine line to toe, and there are no guidebooks on whose advice you should carefully consider and whose you should immediately disregard. It's up to you to make that judgment. One thing to keep in mind, of all the advice you'll receive: none of it is a permanent contract. It's words told to you from someone who believes they're helping you out based on their life experiences, just as this book is based on mine. If it isn't working for you, stop relying on it and try somebody else's advice, or listen to your own voice and see where that takes you.

IMMERSE

"When you are just existing, life happens to you . . . and you manage; when you are truly living, you happen to life . . . and you lead."

—Steve Maraboli

What do I mean, exactly, when I say you need to immerse yourself in the world around you? I mean put your damn video game controller down; shut the TV off; quit consuming news all day; get off your phone; step out of the bars, clubs, and casinos; get up from the couch; and go outside. Walk around in the fresh air and listen to some good music or a podcast or some freaking birds, or simply observe mostly well-meaning humans coexisting in the world around you. Sit down in a park or a coffee shop and read a personal development book. Go somewhere that inspires you, and do some reflecting and writing about the questions I ask you in the guide that accompanies this book. Go for a run, lift some weights, help a family member or friend with something, volunteer at a local school, go for a walk, or find someone to give this book to. Send me an email about whatever is on your mind. (I promise to reply.) Find some friends who always make you feel good and encourage you to do better, and go spend time with them.

It might seem dumb, even useless, to do some of these things, but simply being around other people will help you stay out of your own head and focus on more productive, positive thoughts. I've mentioned maybe ten things, but there are endless things you can go do that are better than sitting on your couch or lying in bed and feeling sorry for yourself, even though I know exactly what that feels like when that's the only thing you want to do. You know that your life is only ever going to get better if you do something about it. Quit telling yourself that someone is going to come in and save you. That's not going to happen!

Start now, and change up the horrendous routine you've allowed into your life. Dive into the world around you. Don't let your reality be shaped by the news, by your social media feed, by people who only believe in one recipe for success, by people who've never done anything with their life. Go out and shape your own reality; one that will slowly but surely begin creating a better, more positive, optimistic outlook for your future. It's within your control, and this is the permission you need to go out and do exactly that.

PARTING WORDS
OF ENCOURAGEMENT

Making it through this book entirely is a small victory in and of itself. You picked it up because something about it intrigued you. Maybe you were lost and without clear guidance on where to go next. Maybe your pain had become unbearable and the subtitle appealed to you. Maybe, much like myself, you have always known there was more for your life than what everyone else around you was saying, doing, and believing, but you weren't sure how to escape it and live authentically. Use my story as a guide in navigating the often messy path of going from where you are to where you want to be, but don't do this alone. That's not how life was meant to be experienced. Join our Facebook group; simply search for Sologood Self Mastery Community—a community of incredible people who also know there's much more for our lives.

Also, if you haven't already and you're looking to take things a bit further, to multiply your chances of living a life that matters, I highly suggest you download the guide which accompanies this book. It's filled with questions that will force you to honestly examine your choices, actions, and outcomes, as well as resources that will surely accelerate your journey towards where you want to be. It can be found at www.sologood.co/bookresources

We all know that life was meant to be enjoyed. Let the choices you make from this point forward move you closer to the future you desire rather than further from it. I wish I could reach through this book right now and give you the biggest hug of appreciation for taking the time to read it and committing to live a better life. I wish I could give you a hug to let you know that I truly care and I want you to move toward a life that matters. I wish I could give you a hug if only to let you know that you matter to me and that your story is powerful beyond measure. I hope that if we ever have the chance to meet you'll come say hi and claim that hug.

As you set this book down, don't let that be the end of your work toward the life you desire. Many of the words in this book will fade from memory. Most of your motivation extracted from it will entirely diminish. Nearly all of my lessons and guidance between the two covers of this book will either be reaffirmed or rejected by the work you do from this point forward.

When the back cover of this book closes, let it signify the official gunshot at the starting line of the marathon you will be running to go from where you are to where you want to be. Let the marathon metaphor remain at the top of your mind as you take two steps forward and most likely fall a step or two back. It's all part of the process. Some days you'll pass five people and feel like you could change the entire world with a snap of your fingers. Other days you'll fall to the ground, become dehydrated, need to tie your shoes, and have to massage a cramp, all the while doing your best to remain on the path to a meaningful and fulfilling life.

It's those bumps and bruises along the way, as you've learned throughout my story and your own experiences, that will allow you to use your adversity as a tool and not a crutch or a weight that holds you back. I want you to realize and truly believe that whether you've been going through something for five days, five months, or five years, you have so much valuable life left ahead of you. It'll take a lot of work and belief in yourself, but it's more than worth it.

You can walk, you can crawl, you can even fall backward, but you can never give up. I believe that as long as you keep trudging through the hard times, with the desire and hope that they will one day get better, you'll eventually make it to where you want to be. After all, that's pretty much what I did, because I didn't know the lessons I share with you in this book until after I made it past all of it.

With that being said: Get UP, and get going!

ACKNOWLEDGMENTS

The only person I could appropriately begin by thanking would be my wife, Brittany. If it weren't for her this book might not have ever existed. Not only because she initiated the idea of beginning to write it in the first place, but also because she has consistently forced me to be honest with myself about my choices from the very beginning. She challenged me to question old beliefs and replace them with healthier, more productive ones. She, in all her beauty, strength, and confidence, allowed me to fully believe that there was more to life than what I had grown accustomed to. She drives me to be a better person in all areas of life by just being who she is. She makes me proud to call her my wife daily and excited for our future endeavors. She is everything I am not, and then some, and for that, I am grateful.

To my two beautiful boys, Cameron and Sully. Their innate curiosity and glistening eyes in the face of wonder and adventure inspire me to never truly "grow up." Whether we're simply goofing around, cooking dinner together, playing outside, or traveling to places new and old, I enjoy nothing more than the privilege of experiencing their awe and wonder of this life they've been given. To say that they're the greatest teacher I've ever had, that they encourage me to question everything, to always look for ways to brighten someone's day, and to love unconditionally, is an understatement. They are my guides for journeying to where I want to be, and also for how I want to be remembered when that hourglass runs out.

To the two people who made all of this possible: my mom and dad. They gave me everything I could have ever wanted out of a childhood. I'm forever grateful for and indebted to the beautiful memories I get to carry with me for the rest of my life. They have been the perfect balance for what I needed throughout my life; my mom for the tough love, grit, and drive to always be a good friend to others and human being in general, and my dad for the listening ear, loving advice, and moral guidance for the poor choices I made. They, along with my incredible step-parents, put up with more than any parent should have to, and through that, taught me a great deal about patience, unconditional love, and the challenges of raising your babies into young men and women.

For my brothers, thank you for often being there when I was going through some difficult times and needed someone to talk to—often, only a brother's ears are safe for listening, and advice is relevant enough to warrant credibility. Although our paths are often as different as could be, I look forward to many more years of growing together and sharing in the joy of watching our kids become young men and women we're proud to call our own.

If it weren't for my in-laws supporting me from almost the first time I met them, marrying my wife might not have been possible. I will be forever grateful for that support when almost any other family might have told me to get lost. They're incredible, loving people who live for adventure, and ensure there's plenty of fun in life—a reminder I need often in order to pull away from my own ambitions to enjoy the simple, finer things in life. An extra thanks to my father-in-law for being such a prime example for how to shower your kids with love and for being honest when confronting me the morning after my drunken outrage following mine and Britt's wedding shower.

To the only friend I had who realized that my potential and my future were worth more than a wild night of drinks out at the bar. A guy who always had my back and gave me the best gift I could've ever received when I most needed it: honesty. He's a guy you want on your side and someone you hope your own kids turn out to be like. He's the kind of person you wish we could clone more of and spread throughout the earth. And although that's all true, he'll probably read this and think he's just a normal guy. His love for me and belief in who I could become is the definition of the quote, "You have not lived until you have done something for someone who can never repay you." This defines him, as I will forever be indebted to him for his belief in me.

To every single person I have crossed paths with throughout my life; whether it be as friends for a summer, a casual conversation at a bar, a smile on the sidewalk, a local in a foreign land, the many military members I've served with, or any other individual significant enough to have spent a few moments on this spinning rock we call earth, which is all of you, I sincerely thank you for sharing with me that which makes life beautiful—your unique differences, diversity, and individual story and gifts.

Finally, I can't thank the team at Wise Ink Publishing for their guidance and support in helping me take my initial 276 pages of jumbled words spread across two notebooks and turning it into the book you now hold I'm your hands. Am extra special thanks to Amy Quale for her ability to ask thoughtful yet difficult questions, which helped to make my story something you would actually want to read. I'm happy I was introduced to them, because without their skills, I'd still be working on this dang thing.

ABOUT THE AUTHOR

Possessed by an insatiable curiosity and drive to help people, Jake Widmann is committed to sharing his own story and the stories of others. If he's not spending time with his wife, Brittany, and his two boys, Cameron and Sully, he's likely drinking coffee while overanalyzing some aspect of his brand, Sologood.co.

If you have a feeling that there's more for your life, reach out to Jake at jake@sologood.co, see what he's doing over at Sologood.co, or join the Sologood Self Mastery Community on Facebook.